T0151786

SOBER & OUT

Lesbian, gay, bisexual and transgender AA members share their experience, strength and hope

———

Stories from AA Grapevine

Books Published by AA Grapevine, Inc.

The Language of the Heart (& eBook)
The Best of Bill (& eBook)
Spiritual Awakenings (& eBook)
I Am Responsible: The Hand of AA
The Home Group: Heartbeat of AA (& eBook)
Emotional Sobriety: The Next Frontier (& eBook)
Spiritual Awakenings II (& eBook)
In Our Own Words: Stories of Young AAs in Recovery (& eBook)
Beginners' Book (& eBook)
Voices of Long-Term Sobriety (& eBook)
A Rabbit Walks into a Bar
Step by Step: Real AAs, Real Recovery (& eBook)
Emotional Sobriety II: The Next Frontier (& eBook)
Young & Sober (& eBook)
Into Action (& eBook)
Happy, Joyous & Free (& eBook)
One on One (& eBook)
The Best of the Grapevine, Volume I (eBook only)
No Matter What (& eBook)
Grapevine Daily Quote Book (& eBook)

IN SPANISH

El Lenguaje del Corazón
Lo Mejor de Bill (& eBook)
Lo Mejor de La Viña
El Grupo Base: Corazón de AA

IN FRENCH

Les meilleurs articles de Bill
Le Langage du coeur
Le Groupe d'attache: Le battement du coeur des AA
En Tête À Tête (& eBook)

SOBER & OUT

Lesbian, gay, bisexual and transgender AA members share their experience, strength and hope

---

Stories from AA Grapevine

AAGRAPEVINE, Inc.

New York, New York

WWW.AAGRAPEVINE.ORG

AA PREAMBLE

Alcoholics Anonymous is a fellowship of men and women
who share their experience, strength and hope
with each other that they may solve their common problem
and help others to recover from alcoholism.

The only requirement for membership is a desire to stop
drinking. There are no dues or fees for AA membership;
we are self-supporting through our own contributions. AA
is not allied with any sect, denomination, politics,
organization or institution; does not wish to engage in any
controversy, neither endorses nor opposes any causes.

Our primary purpose is to stay sober
and help other alcoholics to achieve sobriety.

©AA Grapevine, Inc.

CONTENTS

AA Preamble V
Welcome XI

CHAPTER ONE
AM I AN ALCOHOLIC?

What it was like for LGBT AAs and how they reached out for recovery 1
Risking the Truth *February 1987* 2
Sunlight and Air *May 1999* 4
Condemned to Live an Underground Life *July 1976* 9
I Have Found Myself *August 1982* 13
To Thine Own Self Be True *February 2003* 13

CHAPTER TWO
I FOUND MY FELLOWSHIP

Voices of lesbian AAs 15
Janet's Story *August 2000* 16
Back to Basics *October 1999* 19
Thirsty for Life *July 1986* 21
The Freedom to Belong *January 1983* 22
On Dangerous Ground *February 2011* 24

CHAPTER THREE
HOME AT LAST

Voices of gay male AAs 29
At Home in AA *November 1992* 30
The Topic Is Change *February 2001* 30
The Third Eye *March 1994* 33
Facing Fear *April 2001* 36
Addressing the Wound *May 2008* 37
In Defense of Special Groups *October 1982* 40
In the Center of Sorrow *February 2007* 40

CHAPTER FOUR
FEELING DIFFERENT

Transgender, bisexual and other AAs discuss acceptance, uniqueness and alcoholism 45

Welcome to the Big Top *April 2004*....................................46
Double Trouble *March 2005* 49
Firm Bedrock *May 1999*..52
Rigorous Honesty *June 1982*...54
Stand Fast *June 2011* 55
Whose Rules? *October 2011* 56
Above All, an Alcoholic *September 1982* 56
A Minority of One *October 1997* 59
One Size Fits All *August 1982* 61

CHAPTER FIVE
ROOM FOR ALL OF US

Finding acceptance, love and guidance in the Fellowship................. 63

Quiet Guidance *May 1990* 64
Fitting In *December 1988* 70
Love and Tolerance *October 2000* 71
The Only Requirement *May 1975*......................................72
No Boundaries, Please *July 1987* 73
The Rabbit Hole *August 2003* 74

CHAPTER SIX
LOVE AND TOLERANCE

Dealing with judgment and lack of acceptance, these AAs looked for answers.. 79

Pass the Tissues, I've Got Issues *February 1997*.......................80
Whom Do You Hate? *January 2002*....................................82
A Plea for Love and Tolerance *April 1999* 83
I Want to Belong *October 1977* 84
Special Groups *February 1981*...86
The Support We All Need *January 1980* 86
One Primary Purpose *August 1997* 89
Just How Welcome Are You? *June 1996* 89
A Rare Value *October 2000* 91
Is Our Message for Everyone? *October 1991*..........................92
Response to "Is Our Message for Everyone?" *February 1992* 93

CHAPTER SEVEN
LIFE ON LIFE'S TERMS

Using the Twelve Steps and the Fellowship to deal with adversity,
illness and loss 95
A Death in the Family *February 2004* 96
Staying Sober—No Matter What *July 1992* 98
Here I Am *February 1976.* 101
The Gift that Never Dies *August 2006* 103
Sober at 63 *April 2010.* 108

CHAPTER EIGHT
ENJOYING LIFE MORE THAN EVER BEFORE

The joy of living through working the AA program. 111
In All Our Affairs *April 2005* 112
Fear, Suspicion, Distrust *May 1988* 114
The Best of Times *July 2007* 115
In Diversity Is Strength *April 1982* 116
Acceptance Is a Two-Way Street *April 1985* 118
Special Interest Groups? *April 1989* 121
Love and Tolerance *November 1996* 122
There Is Only One AA *November 1984* 124
You Are Not Done Yet *March 2009* 125

Twelve Steps 130
Twelve Traditions 131
About AA and AA Grapevine 132

WELCOME

S*ober & Out* is a collection of Grapevine stories written primarily by alcoholics who are lesbian, gay, bisexual and transgendered (LGBT) members of AA. Here, along with stories from some other AA friends, they share their experience, strength and hope in recovery, as well as their personal struggles and their hard-fought triumphs.

Getting sober for any alcoholic can be difficult and the stories in this book show that—like most alcoholics—lesbian, gay, bisexual and transgender AAs struggle to fit in, to stay sober and to find peace in their lives. Yet, by working the Steps, following the Traditions, doing service and finding a Higher Power, they are now living sober in the Fellowship of AA.

Alcoholism can be a lonely business, and AA has always sought to be inclusive in its membership, keeping its doors open for alcoholics of every description. As stated in AA's Preamble, "The only requirement for membership is a desire to stop drinking." And, while the LGBT members whose stories appear in this volume clearly meet that requirement, many have also faced challenges of acceptance and discrimination in getting sober. Some turned to the support, identification and understanding found in special-interest AA meetings with other LGBT members, though most have also found that attending regular meetings has helped to broaden and deepen their experience of recovery. Says one member, "When I hear the terms 'straight AA' or 'gay AA,' I cringe. There is only one AA, 'a fellowship of men and women who share their experience, strength and hope with each other that they may solve their common problem and help others to recover from alcoholism.'"

While Grapevine has long been an avenue of expression for the individual stories of AA members, many LGBT members have been hesitant to share their experience, strength and hope openly in meetings, fearing rejection or judgment. However, more often than not, these fears have been unfounded and AA's primary purpose has shone through. As one AA explains, "When I told my sponsor I am a lesbian, she said, 'So what? You want to get sober, don't you?'"

Ultimately, these AAs discovered that recovery from alcoholism is more important than their sexual orientation and that by staying sober and following AA's program of recovery, full and purposeful lives could be built, one day at a time.

CHAPTER 1

AM I AN ALCOHOLIC?

What it was like for LGBT AAs and how they reached out for recovery

Every alcoholic in recovery travels their own path to the doors of AA. The authors in this chapter are lesbian, gay, bisexual or transgender. Some didn't realize their sexual orientation until after getting sober. Others knew who they were but were reluctant to share. But all found they had to be honest about themselves in order to stay sober.

Getting honest for any AA can be difficult, but it is worth it, writes one AA, recognizing "that somewhere among the readership of this magazine there are other persons like me, as I once was—shakily sober, but still living in guilt and the indescribable fear that homosexuality will prove to be an insurmountable obstacle in the path of sobriety and happiness. Have hope, my unknown friends," he says. "You can be happy and live a useful life."

The stories in this chapter show how gay and lesbian alcoholics recognized their alcoholism and—quickly or slowly—reached out for recovery and began to accept themselves and become part of the AA Fellowship.

Risking the Truth
FEBRUARY 1987

In Alcoholics Anonymous the importance of identification and honest sharing cannot be overemphasized. When I arrived at the doors of AA, I was isolated, frightened, and convinced that life would never improve. I had a vague hope that there could be something in AA for me—something that could make a sober and drug free life perhaps bearable—but I was not convinced. I have certainly found that "something," however, and much more, but only over a period of years and with much soul-searching through inventory and risk-taking through honest sharing.

It seems that so many of us on entering AA have our own reasons why the program will not work. If one is married, it is because of a truculent spouse. If one is single, it is because there is no supportive partner. If one is employed, it is due to a demanding, overbearing boss. If one is unemployed, it's due to the lack of funds. In my case I was gay. No one would want me in meetings and even if I were tolerated there, I would not be allowed to speak of my lifestyle. And if I did *listen* in meetings, the identification would not be present for me.

Two statements in our literature flash in my mind at this point. One is in the book *Alcoholics Anonymous*. "Burn the idea into the consciousness of every man that he can get well regardless of anyone. The only condition is that he trust in God and clean house." The second statement is from the pamphlet "A Member's Eye View of Alcoholics Anonymous." "I am personally convinced that the basic search of every human being, from the cradle to the grave, is to find at least one other human being before whom he can stand completely naked, stripped of all pretense or defense, and trust that person not to hurt him, because that other person has stripped himself naked, too. This lifelong search can begin and end with the first AA encounter." These, and many other statements in AA literature, gave me the hope that AA might work for me.

After I had about six weeks of sobriety, I talked with a man who had many years of sobriety. He told me that if there were anything standing between me and my God, I must get rid of it or risk drinking again. He also said that a man could not act contrary to his particular nature and remain comfortable. Each of us interprets such things differently, depending upon his or her emotional and spiritual status at the time, and I interpreted them as meaning that I must be stark raving heterosexual, and happy with it! I threw myself wholeheartedly into the AA program, my marriage, and my work, expecting that the "cure" would happen at any moment. I became so busy with work, meetings, inventories, housing and furnishings for my family, having children and raising them that I had no time to discover me. Finally, after about three years of frenzied sobriety, I slowed down enough to get in contact with me—with my sadness and emptiness caused by trying to be someone other than who I was. (Really, trying to be who I thought you wanted me to be.)

Because of the pain involved in my self-discovery, I was forced to talk in AA meetings about who I really was, and slowly, over several years, I have discovered a beautiful human being inside this skin. I had to let go of the notion that everyone must like me or approve of my lifestyle. I also needed to realize that when speaking in AA meetings, I must be honest but sensitive to the feelings of others. I had to learn to use the telephone for "one-on-one" conversations, but when my sobriety was at stake, I could not be deterred from honest and open sharing in meetings. (I defend the right of any member of AA to talk in an AA meeting about anything *he* feels is necessary to keep him from taking a drink.)

Old-timers in AA repeatedly told me that when I became comfortable with me, others would become comfortable with me as well. I find that to be true today. Much has transpired over the last seven and one-half years of my sobriety and abstinence from mind-altering chemicals. I have a very close relationship with my children and my ex-wife, closer than was ever possible when we lived together. We see one another often in a spirit of openness and honesty. I do not hide my homosexuality from my children. Likewise, they have expressed their concerns to me and we deal with our feelings completely "up front."

My relationships in the gay community are wholesome, loving, dignified. I have had the opportunity to help several gay friends become involved in AA. They are now beginning the journey which I began. They would not have had the identification necessary to begin this journey had someone not been willing to take a risk and be honest and open in an AA meeting.

Finally, I have found in my own way that AA is my solution for sober living. The Steps work in my life for all sorts of problems. In meetings I identify with nearly every person who shares—we are all alcoholics and have similar feelings even though the details of our experience may differ. I listen now to the heart, from the heart. I have learned to trust that God, as I understand him, loves me just as he made me. I walk in life everywhere—at home, at work, in and out of AA—with my head up high, grateful for the inner peace which God has given me through AA.

M. B.
Cardiff by the Sea, California

Sunlight and Air
MAY 1999

I came to Alcoholics Anonymous young in years but sick of soul and full of secrets. Now, in my middle age, I no longer harbor secrets, and my soul is in better health than ever. It's freer, more generous, and able as it never was in my drinking days to receive love and joy and wonder as well as the darker emotions.

While all of AA's twelve suggested Steps are crucial to my ongoing recovery, the Fifth Step more than any other has helped me get free of those soul-crippling secrets.

I attended my first AA meetings with my then-partner. She was older than I, and her alcoholism was more visible. When our physician prescribed AA for her, I went along because, except for our jobs and her occasional disappearing acts during binges, we did everything as a unit. I realize now that I didn't trust her to go on her own. I didn't trust AA either, and knew next to nothing about it. How could those people understand her the way I did?

The first meeting we stumbled (!) into was open to all. I hastened to explain to the group members who greeted us that my partner was the one with the problem; I was just there for moral support. They told me about Al-Anon but said I was welcome at open AA meetings, too. Much as I did need Al-Anon, it was open AA meetings that saved my life.

My partner and I went together to several open meetings a week. We still drank, though, and I still flew into rages and battered her insensible during our drunken arguments, sometimes so badly that we ended the night in a hospital emergency room. These outbursts, I told myself, were caused by her drunkenness. Who wouldn't lose patience with such obnoxious behavior?

At AA meetings, I listened only for what might get my partner sober, but after hearing scores of alcoholics tell their stories, I couldn't help but look at my own drinking. I didn't consider myself an alcoholic—after all, I wasn't as bad off as her—but it did come through to me that normal social drinking did not result in blackouts or fits of violence or the need to drive with one eye closed to keep from seeing two sets of lines in the middle of the road.

At that time, I was a newspaper reporter. My beat was a rural county that voted with paper ballots, and on election nights all the reporters who covered the county brought food and soft drinks to the county clerk's office to share while we waited out the vote tally and then wrote our stories. I had my last drink on an election night when I had decided that my contribution would be a case of beer. No one else ever brought alcohol, nor had anyone suggested that I bring it. Every time I helped myself to one of the beers, I urged others to join me, but they all declined, saying they needed their wits about them while there was work to be done. I defiantly drank several more beers, somehow wrote my stories, and drove myself home without incident—hardly high drama compared to the drunken domestic battles. The next day nevertheless found me face-to-face with the realization that while my colleagues had focused on their work, I had been obsessed with the beer. AA had ruined my drinking! I still couldn't admit that I was an alcoholic, but I doubt now that I could have stopped drinking or stayed stopped without the support I got secretly from attending AA meetings as a spectator.

My partner and I eventually separated, and I no longer had a reason to attend AA meetings—or so I thought. I moved to the city, where I was heartsick and achingly lonely—although I kept that a secret even from myself—but also painfully self-conscious and fearful of meeting people. A few drinks would make all this easier, I thought, and maybe I could drink moderately now that I knew the danger signs. Fortunately, my closest friend was a sober alcoholic I had met at one of those open meetings. Before I resumed drinking, she gently guided me back to AA, suggesting that if I listened for myself this time I just might discover that I belonged here. She told me that the only requirement for membership was a desire to stop drinking, and that I was entitled to the help that AA provides for living without alcohol.

Almost immediately, I accepted the First Step and declared myself an alcoholic, which brought a great sense of relief. I set about working the rest of the Steps, too, but I secretly edited them because I didn't believe in God. People who did, I thought, were just too weak-minded to face hard reality. I would use AA to restore myself to sanity. I would turn my life over to the care of ... well, AA would do as a Higher Power. My first attempt at a Fourth Step produced a list of my drunken misdeeds, and for my Fifth Step, I recited this list to the sponsor I rarely saw or called, tossing in an amusing detail added here and there to keep her attention. And so on. I went to lots of meetings, but I barely skimmed the surface of the Steps, and above all I avoided close examination of my own soul and any mention of God. My secrets stayed secret, and I stayed sick.

Eventually, meetings began to irritate me. I looked around the rooms and focused on the few sober alcoholics whose lives seemed marginal to me and decided it was crazy to depend on them for guidance. Besides, I had a new partner, who was not an alcoholic, and my life was manageable now. Maybe it was a mistake, I thought, to define myself in terms of a disease. Coping without alcohol no longer seemed difficult. I concluded that I could stop attending meetings and stay sober with the other tools AA had given me.

In truth, I had little real practice with most of those other tools. My moral inventory had been neither fearless nor searching. I had never admitted my most serious shortcomings to myself, let alone to another person or to the God I didn't believe in. The self-centered fears and resentments I had carried through my drinking and into sobriety were still with me, because I could not remove them myself and was far from ready for God to remove them. Now, without meetings and fellowship with other recovering alcoholics to subdue them, my character defects took on new strength.

Any veneer of emotional sobriety I might have developed quickly wore away once I stopped going to meetings. I didn't beat my new partner—at least I hadn't hit anyone since I'd stopped drinking—but I did try to control her every breath and showed no respect for her feelings. My frequent outbursts of obsessive jealousy left me humiliated and ashamed, and so did the romantic obsession I developed with another woman that led me to betray my partner. When my escalating emotional turmoil kept me from concentrating on my work, I made serious mistakes that cost me a job and increased my sense of shame. I had not picked up a drink yet, but emotionally I was worse off than ever. Finally, when I hit what I now know was a spiritual bottom, I went back to the one place that

I knew would still welcome me—AA meetings.

This time I was ready to open my mind and my heart to the program in its entirety, to seek serenity and emotional sobriety and not just the quick fix. Now when I looked around the rooms, I focused on people who had what I wanted. I saw that they were the ones who worked at improving their conscious contact with God as they understood Him—or Her, or It. I still couldn't claim even the slightest knowledge of God, but it was clear to me at last that I needed to depend on something much bigger than me. Even AA couldn't fill that bill, because it was made up of people like me. My understanding of a Higher Power is still subject to shifts. Sometimes, I think of it as The Unknowable, or as The Great What Is. Often, I envision it as an indifferent force, something like an electrical current, that is available to all living things and from which human beings can derive strength and generosity and acceptance. The one thing I feel sure of is that it's more powerful than my will or any mere human or collection of humans, even AA as a whole; that's what makes it higher.

Having acknowledged a Higher Power, regardless of how little I understood of its nature, I was ready at last to take the Steps of AA as they are and not as I wished them to be. For starters, I saw that I had not restored myself to sanity, and that I never could. All the Steps seemed different now, including those that don't specifically mention a Higher Power.

The Fourth Step, to me, is like a tour of a haunted house. My first time around, when I heard the scuttling in the walls, I raced alone through the hallways and out the back door. This time, the acceptance of a Higher Power gave me the courage to open the closet doors and even venture into the cellar. I found long-hidden stores of fear and resentment. I found a few hidden treasures, too.

Having uncovered my character defects, I could admit the exact nature of my wrongs, not just their most obvious manifestations. The hardest part of the Fifth Step was admitting the truth to myself. I had to look at the fears and insecurities that led me to hurt that former partner in many ways, not just physically, to harass and betray my current partner, and to hurt others I loved as well. I preferred to see myself as an unfailingly generous friend who had pulled myself up by my bootstraps, required little from others, and never gave in to self-pity. Instead, I had to admit that my need for the love and approval of others felt bottomless, that I deeply envied my friends' achievements, and that I blamed the deprivations of my childhood for my own failure to rise above the level of mediocrity. Admitting these character defects to my Higher Power was easier than admitting them to myself, because my understanding of God has nothing to do with judgment and everything to do with the acceptance of what is. Once I felt secure in the acceptance of a Higher Power, admitting the truth about myself to another human being seemed much less risky.

If the Fourth Step is the exploration of an abandoned house, I have come to think of the Fifth Step as raising the blinds and throwing open the windows. The house has air and sunlight now, and it's no longer haunted. When people come to the door, I can welcome them without shame, and I can even invite them in. Some rooms are private of course, but none are secret, and I live in all of them.

Cheryl M.
New York, New York

Condemned to Live an Underground Life

JULY 1976

The group was a medium-sized one in a residential suburb of a large Western city. It was the weekly speaker meeting, and I was introduced as "one of our younger members from the __ Group."

I stood up, identified myself as an alcoholic, and launched into the story of what I used to be like, what happened, and what I'm like now. Well, *almost*. For there is a vital part of my story that I could not and would not tell those fine people.

"I am an alcoholic, *and* I am a practicing homosexual. I don't look it; I don't mince when I walk or wear outlandish clothes; I don't go around the room after the meeting soliciting good-looking male AAs. But the fact remains, I am a practicing homosexual." I've often speculated on the reactions of those people had I made that statement and told them the parts of my past and present that I left out or glossed over in my pitch.

For that matter, what would *your* reaction be?

Throughout the darkest depths of my drinking, I tried desperately to come to terms with the fact that I was a homosexual, a member of a minority group looked upon by great segments of society as "revolting," "disgusting," "unnatural," "queer." I lived in a triple world: the facade of a normal man; the self-abasement of alcoholic drinking; the secret knowledge of my homosexuality.

Toward the end, quantities of booze would wash away the barriers between the worlds, and I would go on a wild, alcoholic trip, motivated by my desire to be with others like me. It always ended in disaster. One trip ended in my discharge from the service as "undesirable"; another caused untold embarrassment and heartache for my family and the firm that then employed me.

No matter how hard I tried, I sank deeper and deeper into the guilt-filled whirlpool of alcohol and sexual desire. Then, one day, alcohol became the most important thing. I was drinking to be drinking, not to numb the inhibitions of social behavior so I could be what I really wanted to be. My homosexual companions and friends rejected me as an untrustworthy drunk who might give away their own secret. Several of them tried to protect me from what seemed to be eventual self-destruction. This time, I rejected them—the very people I wanted to be with. I was really all alone.

I had tried AA several times, each time for a different physical or material reason. When sober in those periods, I put on a bright mask of confidence, but I lived in fear and frustration. I got no-where with AA. I couldn't be totally honest with myself or anyone else. I was a homosexual. So I found myself utterly alone in the world, a lousy "drunken queer."

But something changed. I wanted to get sober, because I want-ed to be sober more than I wanted to drink. I went to the AA office and club in a daze, hoping that somehow, somewhere, I could get sober and stay sober. For the very first time, I asked my Higher Power to help me get sober and stay sober.

But the specter of my homosexuality was still there. "Sure, you're sober in AA again. That's nothing new," I said to myself. Then came the burning question: "But how are you going to ac-cept the fact that you're a homosexual and, as such, must always be condemned to living an underground life, *even with your AA comrades?*"

At first, I concentrated strictly on staying sober and attending meetings. I said nothing to anyone about my "other" life. I asked the Higher Power each day to show me the way to a solution. About a month or two after I came on the program, I met another homosexual, a man much older in years and sobriety than I. One Sunday afternoon, we drove out of town to an institution to see an AA inmate. Without actually realizing I was doing it, I told this man my *real* story and told him how desperate I was to stay sober and be able to make a life for myself. I was breathless with apprehension and fear, but I *had* to tell it.

When I finished, he glanced at me with a smile on his face and said, "Welcome to AA." He told me then several things I'll never for-get. The first was that it was possible to stay sober and live the life of a homosexual. There were others in the AA program; I would meet them in time. He said to me, "You didn't ask to be a homo-sexual, but you *are.* Short of long, difficult, and expensive psychi-atric treatment, there is little chance that you can change your sexual life and desires, *even if you wanted to.* Your Higher Power knows what you are, and so do I. Your job now is to learn to live with your homosexuality, to make the best of a difficult bargain."

What a great day! I had a glimmer of hope for the first time in many years. Here was someone who understood my life, someone who knew *exactly* how I felt. It was as if a whole new life had begun. I knew it was possible to be myself and stay sober!

That was over ten years ago, and I wish I could honestly report that life has been smooth and calm since then. But, of course, that isn't true. It took months of difficult inventory-taking and many wild, emotional discussions to accept the fact that I was a homosexual. It took a couple of years of fearful experimentation to discover that I could lead—for me—a normal life. What is normal for me sexually is totally repugnant to the majority of people. But I have to live basically for me if I am to continue to stay sober and work this program. There have been many periods of terrible doubt and darkness, periods when I've sincerely questioned whether I could continue to lead the kind of life I lead.

But my Higher Power and the truth and wisdom of the AA way of life have given me the means to continue to grow as a person and a useful, sober member of society. I do my share of Twelfth Step work, with both heterosexual and homosexual people. I don't force my homosexuality on them. My interest is in their drinking problem. The Higher Power has enabled me to be, for me, extremely objective when working with a newcomer. I have hundreds of heterosexual friends in AA and many, many homosexual ones. Many, of both kinds, have no idea that I am a homosexual. Others know, understand, and aren't interested in my friendship for its sexual aspects.

In writing this, I am thinking that somewhere among the readership of this magazine there are other persons like me, as I once was—shakily sober, but still living in guilt and the indescribable fear that their homosexuality will prove to be an insurmountable obstacle in the path of sobriety and happiness. Have hope, my unknown friends! You *can* be happy and live a useful life. Two suggestions I might make: (1) Remember you're an alcoholic first and a homosexual second, and (2) ask *your* Higher Power for guidance and help. It's there, and it'll come to you if you sincerely want it!

B. L.
Manhattan, New York

I Have Found Myself
AUGUST 1982 *(From Dear Grapevine)*

Thank you very much for the April Grapevine article "In Diversity Is Strength."

Thanks to my God and to people who understand and are accepting of others, I came to realize (after I had been sober for two and a half years) that I am gay. Gay people really do have the same desire to stay sober and help other alcoholics—gay or straight—to achieve sobriety as do the straight members.

I now have over six years' sobriety. I owe my sobriety to God and to all the straight meetings I attend, because there are no gay meetings in my hometown. I work the Steps and try to practice the principles in all my affairs, as do other alcoholics who want a contented sobriety. I have found myself through the AA Fellowship.

Anonymous
Kansas

To Thine Own Self Be True
FEBRUARY 2003

Self-concern and fear dominated me most of my life. I was also afraid that people could detect my fear so I drank to escape it and to escape from myself. When I was sober for two and a half years, I realized that the quality of my life left me wanting. I was still very self-conscious and full of fear.

Ill at ease in meetings, I decided to cut back on them. But I soon realized that fewer meetings couldn't possibly be the right answer. I decided to take a deeper look into myself. Why was I so self-conscious and full of fear all the time, no matter whom I was with or where I was?

One day it dawned on me that my self-perception was so distorted that I couldn't possibly live up to the person I was pretending to be because that person didn't exist. Because of my religious background, I had not been able to admit that I was gay. So I had lived a lie my entire life. The result was terror, bewilderment, frustration, and despair.

When I got sick and tired of being "sober and miserable," I realized that my problem was deeper than alcoholism. My problem was sexual confusion. My alcoholism was merely a symptom.

The words "and we have ceased fighting anything or anyone— even alcohol" finally rang true for me. Ever since I was a child, I had modified everything about myself, from the way I walked, to the way I talked, to the way I dressed. And I was still a misfit. Thanks to AA, I don't have to fight any longer.

Shakespeare said, "To thine own self be true." He didn't say be someone you aren't. Today I am alcohol-free. I am what I am—a sober gay man!

Steve C.
College Park, Maryland

CHAPTER 2

I FOUND MY FELLOWSHIP

Voices of lesbian AAs

M ost of the womens' stories in this chapter deal with drinking and self-acceptance.

"At twenty-one years old, I became aware of bars for lesbians, and this was the discovery of my life," F.G. writes. "I started to go to these bars, and since I had already developed a dependence on alcohol, I drank. Alcohol became my way of life." Liquor "made my feelings of inferiority ... disappear," writes Janet W. "I felt as if I had found the answer to my problems."

Finally reaching Alcoholics Anonymous, these women found help through sponsors, new friends in the rooms, and reliance on a Higher Power.

One AA, Linda W., writes that the members of her group "were the embodiment of Tradition Three. It didn't matter that I was a nurse in the intensive care unit, or that I was a lesbian. I was there for the same reason they were, to stop drinking and to learn to live sober. I felt supported, cared for, and even loved."

In this chapter, lesbian AAs talk about how the program changed their lives.

Janet's Story
AUGUST 2000

Being an alcoholic and gay were never on my agenda for my life. Far from it, my goal was to become a missionary or at least a minister's wife or parish worker, which was more probable for a young girl at that time. I grew up in a small suburb of Los Angeles during the 1940s. Life centered around the family and church activities and was orderly and peaceful. I played the piano, sang in the junior choir, and had a comforting, childlike faith in God.

I had heard about alcoholism from my grandmother, whose father had been a judge in South Dakota for fifty years, and apparently, a practicing alcoholic. I adopted my family's feelings about drinking and drinkers and knew I would never be like that. Being homosexual, I learned, was also unacceptable. This idea came from many sources—friends, church, movies, and family—and I believed it, happily going my way feeling critical and superior. Once in a while, however, I feared that I had those kinds of feelings, which scared me because I desperately wanted to be a "good girl," and acceptable.

My life changed abruptly and dramatically when I was twelve years old and my father died. My mother remarried soon after, and there was a lot of stress and tension in our family. My stepfather's attempts to take my father's place filled me with resentment, and throughout my childhood I never accepted him or felt he accepted or liked me.

I left home at eighteen to pursue my goal of a church career by attending a Lutheran bible school in Los Angeles. Although I felt close to God there, I continued to feel what I'd felt all through high school: that I was inferior and didn't belong anywhere. Although I tried to fit in, I mostly felt like an outsider. And while I still had very conservative values, I grew increasingly afraid I had homosexual feelings that weren't going away.

At age twenty I went to a small church college in Nebraska where I fell deeply in love—not with that future minister I had always planned to marry, but with a woman. Even though I had feared this, it was now impossible to deny this reality in my life. I was scared, and before the end of the school year I got engaged to an old high school boyfriend to make myself feel as if I were really okay. When I consulted my favorite minister at the bible school, I was told to "pray about it." I did pray a lot, and broke my engagement (fortunately for him). Then I tried dating several other men to see if I could change. Nothing changed, and everything changed. I no longer felt close to God, no longer felt God loved me as I was, and I turned my back on the church and God.

I went back to college, began studying psychology, and grew extremely depressed and often suicidal. It was then that I discovered alcohol. Alcohol, amazingly, made my feelings of inferiority, unacceptability, and shyness disappear. I felt as if I had found the answer to my problems. Alcohol, in conjunction with my many different relationships with women, became my new interest in life and replaced my relationship with God.

After college, I went to Seattle to study for a degree at a school of social work. I had no interest in that profession, but I had a scholarship and wanted to get away from Los Angeles for a while. I did so much drinking there that my family got worried, and a fellow student told me that I was drinking alcoholically. I thought this was ludicrous and continued to drink, enjoying the sense of belonging that alcohol gave me. When I returned to Los Angeles, I continued my pursuit of happiness and security through alcohol and relationships. I had no interest in my profession; in fact, I was scared of the people I was supposed to be helping. I often hid out in my office after a night of drinking, hoping I wouldn't be called on to meet with a family in crisis.

I had my own crisis going on. I had been in what I thought was a monogamous relationship for four years when it suddenly became clear that there was someone else in her life. I didn't have the self-esteem to leave the relationship, so I agreed to share, even going so far as to agree to an every-other-day-together schedule. It was demoralizing and demeaning, and I drank more and more. This turned out to be a blessing in disguise because after a year, the pain of that period in my life turned out to be the impetus that got me to Alcoholics Anonymous.

At the time, I was taking an alcoholic friend to AA to help her. I loved the meetings but considered myself only a visitor. I enjoyed the fellowship, loved the birthdays, and admired newcomers receiving chips for their sobriety. I even wished that I were an alcoholic so I could belong. Then I would go home and read the Big Book while I sipped my wine, never acknowledging that I had a problem. It was Tradition Three that brought me in. Things got so bad in my life I thought that maybe if I stopped drinking for a while I could get it together. Since Tradition Three states that the only require-ment for membership is a desire to stop drinking, I didn't have to be an alcoholic. I did want to stop drinking—for a while anyway. I couldn't imagine how I would ever have any fun or enjoy my life again without drinking. And although I identified myself as an al-coholic at meetings because it was the acceptable thing to do, it took me years of sobriety before I really believed I was an alcoholic.

What I found in Alcoholics Anonymous was, ironically, what I had been looking for all of my life. I found acceptance, love, and support beyond measure, a new definition of my Higher Power, and Twelve Steps to work and follow, which have never let me down in over twenty years of sobriety. I came in feeling that any admission of weakness would make me look bad. What I found out instead was that it is okay to be human!

My definition of God has changed also. I now have a relationship with a God who loves me unconditionally and accepts every part of me just as I am—including my sexuality. Acceptance of myself in this area has brought an end to the struggle and pain of trying to change into something I was not. I now have good friends who have been with me through good and bad times, an unusually support-ive family, and work that I find both satisfying and enjoyable. Pro-fessionally, I coordinate an HIV testing program for children and adolescents, which gives me a feeling of being of service. I am also employed as an organist in a Lutheran church that chooses to be inclusive of all people and is especially welcoming to gays. And for thirteen years, I have been in a relationship with a woman who is a member of Al-Anon. I have found that relationships don't just hap-pen, they require work, commitment, love, the help of good friends, and, most important, an attempt to accept each other as is. We each work our respective programs, and have built a life together around the process of recovery that keeps getting better all the time.

Janet W.
Los Angeles, California

Back to Basics
OCTOBER 1999

sobered up in Fredericton, New Brunswick in August 1997. I am grateful for the two women who came to my apartment when I called the AA line for help. I will always be grateful for them, and for the solid, basic AA knowledge that was instilled into me.

The members in Fredericton taught me that I only had to not drink that first drink. If I didn't drink the first, there would be no second or more. I didn't have to worry about the next bottle, or next drunk, or what would happen tomorrow or next week. I was to live one day at a time. It was not something that I was used to—I used to plan each day months in advance—but quickly understood what was meant.

I can't begin to count the number of times that one day was too much, as was one hour. I remember sitting alone, terrified to go to another member's place, because I'd have to pass a liquor store, and not trusting myself that I *would* pass by. So I sat on my couch, rocking, watching the second hand on my watch, thinking, Thank God, I made it through that minute. I couldn't call anyone. It took a long time before my pride allowed me to call someone, to get a bit of their experience, strength and hope.

They said go to 90 meetings in 90 days. I was pleased with myself. I went to over 120 meetings in 90 days. I was also told I shouldn't start a relationship in my first year. Surely I could have a little affair? I should've listened. When the woman I was involved with left me, I drank. That drunk reinforced that yes, I am an alcoholic, that this is a progressive disease, and that the AA program works, if I work it.

I like to think that I did what I was told (suggested), and for the most part, I did. I even went with a crowd out to a birthday meeting in Stanley, New Brunswick. It was an "eatin' meetin." We had the meeting, the wives of the birthday boys cooked a roast beef dinner for the 70 or so people, then the local boys played down-home country music. I couldn't handle a social scene yet so I escaped to the kitchen and washed dishes. I could focus on simple chores, like washing dishes.

The members in Fredericton were the embodiment of Tradition Three. It didn't matter that I was a nurse in the intensive care unit, or that I was a lesbian. I was there for the same reason they were, to stop drinking and to learn to live sober. I felt supported, cared for, and even loved.

Within a year I relocated across the country. I had my Big Book and "Twelve and Twelve" in my truck with me. I went to meetings in almost every community that I stopped in. If I didn't get to a meeting, I was staying with other women in the program. Within three days of arriving in my new home, I was going to meetings and looking for a sponsor.

I am grateful that I was able to learn so much from the members in Fredericton. I believe that because of them, I stayed sober after my slip during my drive across the country and the first few incredibly stressful months in Victoria. In order to stay sober in Victoria, I had to go back to the basics that I learned in Fredericton: don't drink, go to meetings, get a sponsor.

I am thankful for the members of AA, especially in Fredericton, for they first showed me what sober life can be like, and I do want what they have.

Linda W.
Victoria, British Columbia

Thirsty for Life
JULY 1986

My name is "Frances." I am an alcoholic, drug addict, and lesbian. I had a very difficult childhood, in violence and revolt. I was an unsatisfied, disturbed girl who needed a lot of love.

At the age of eighteen, I got my first full-time job in a drugstore. It was then that I started to take pills on a regular basis. Slowly alcohol came into my life, but only on rare occasions. To be like other women, and mostly because I did not accept my orientation, I started to go out with men. I did not feel good inside. I was not at ease with men, and I needed drugs and alcohol to play the game.

At twenty-one years old, I became aware of bars for lesbians, and this was the discovery of my life. I started to go to these bars, and since I had already developed a dependence on alcohol, I drank. Alcohol became my way of life. As the years went by, my consumption of alcohol increased as the number of my friends decreased. I was contemplating suicide. I was very negative; my heart was full of hatred and I had no motivation whatsoever for any personal life.

One day, I met a woman who carried the AA message to me. I started to attend meetings and stopped taking pills and alcohol. I use the word "attend" because it took me a few months before I really felt that I belonged in AA. It was only by taking on activities such as making coffee, greeting newcomers, chairing a meeting, and being a GSR that I felt I was an AA member.

I then started to work the Steps, and for five years I have not had a drink, a pill, or any other drugs. My life has changed, my way of thinking has changed, and my opinion of life has changed also.

Today, I accept the fact that I am an alcoholic, and that means not to take the first drink, to live the suggested AA program with all my heart. I am happy to be a lesbian; I love my daily work. I am a painter, which is what I have always wanted to be—it was the biggest dream of my alcoholic life.

I love life, I have peace of mind, I live in harmony with myself. I have learned to accept the constraints of life; I now face reality. I am more a woman of action than a woman in reaction, and hope is more present in my life than insecurity.

My heart is full of gratitude and I want this gratitude to stay with me; it is my fountain of life.

As much as I was thirsty for alcohol, today I am thirsty for knowledge, and thirsty to live. My sickness today is ignorance.

F. G.
Montreal, Quebec

The Freedom to Belong
JANUARY 1983

Not long after I started my drinking career, I realized I had a drinking problem. But I kept feeling that if my other problems would go away, I wouldn't drink so much.

Needless to say, the disease of alcoholism was progressing nicely, and I kept thinking that maybe I should go to AA. I am a lesbian. Although I lived in an area with a high population of gays, the closest gay AA meeting available was 150 miles away, in Miami, Florida. I kept seeing articles in magazines about meetings for gays, and pride kept me from going anyplace else, because I condemned people I didn't even know. "They" wouldn't understand me, I believed—part of my disease, I've come to find out.

My disease kept right on progressing until I knew that I could no longer live with myself, that I was at the end of my rope in every circumstance: family, job, friends.

I realized I had to do something and finally gave AA a call one morning. They told me that there was a meeting that night. By the grace of God, I made it to that meeting, though I had gone out all day to celebrate the end of my job career. (It's pretty sick to reach a decision to go to AA and then go out and drink.) I was in a semi-blackout during the meeting. But I was welcomed and asked to come back. I left with a good feeling.

As I started getting sober, I could see that some members really had the sort of recovery I wanted. I finally asked one of the women in the program to be my sponsor. It didn't take long, though, for pride to stand in my way—I wanted nothing to do with the rest of those "idiots." I hadn't come to AA to make friends. I had come because I was desperate. Thank God, I told my sponsor how I felt. She informed me that I would never know the results of the program unless I gave it an honest try.

I now live in an area that holds at least one gay meeting every day of the week, but I don't find it important to make gay meetings only. I find it important to make meetings where the members are serious about the AA program as it is written. To me, it is sad when someone from a minority can feel accepted only in a group of other minority people. This program has given me the freedom to feel that I *belong* in several areas of my life, not just with gays. For this, I am grateful.

I was told from the very beginning to keep an open mind with everyone who walked through the doors of AA. Through attending various meetings, I have learned so much from members who have more sobriety than I.

I guess my point is an idea I try to share with fellow sufferers: This program teaches us first how to "Live," and then we can "Let Live." I need all of you, from every walk of life, to teach me. And I thank each member who, when I came into AA, accepted me for who and what I am.

L. P.
Atlanta, Georgia

On Dangerous Ground
FEBRUARY 2011

Growing up, I felt terminally unique. I made great attempts to be better than most at everything I did—school, work, relationships, etc. There always seemed to be a gap in my ability to conform to what society deemed acceptable. I couldn't stand authority, but was too afraid to rebel. I was afraid of making others angry, so I kept to myself most of the time and became an extreme introvert. I was always trying to be someone or something else, trying to figure out how to be comfortable in my own skin. I felt unacceptable. My drinking played a large part in my search for ease and comfort. I could go away when I drank. I wasn't drinking to get drunk. I just wanted to be happy as myself.

I had hoped, when I got sober, that I would learn how to become comfortable with myself. What I didn't know was where that journey would take me.

My life took a huge turn at five years of sobriety. I decided to change sponsors after we had been working together for four years. I'd worked through the Steps a few times and got some relief each time. But there was always the one thing I could never write down: my deepest, darkest secret I was sure to go to my grave with. This secret was never to see the light of day; it managed to elude all

Fourth and Fifth Steps—and I had no idea what it was. I stayed in bondage because of it for many years. I got married, hoping to make myself and my family happy, only to turn around 14 months later and file for divorce. I thought I had it all—the man, the marriage, the house and the career. I was utterly insane and beginning to die slowly from the "dis-ease" of my alcoholism. In the chaos of divorce and the deluge of questions from my family, I just wanted to hide. This isolation took the form of going to meetings and not speaking, or, if I did speak, putting on a good front and not really sharing what was going on.

My sponsor had said early on that if I felt I was no longer getting what I needed she'd support my moving on. That's exactly what I had come to realize; it was time for me to move on. I started going to some different meetings and met a woman, J., whom I soon asked to sponsor me. I thought that J. had a good program, and I instantly knew I could trust her with my life. I remember sitting in a coffee shop shortly after we started working together, feeling like a failure. I told J. that I couldn't go on living an inauthentic life. I'd come to the jumping-off point the Big Book talks about. I could neither imagine my life as it was, or any other way. What was my choice to be? I couldn't keep living as I'd been doing to this point. I was becoming awakened to all the denial, the dishonesty and the masks I'd been hiding behind since childhood, and I was being exposed with breakneck speed. If ever there was a time in sobriety when I felt like drinking, it was at that moment. I remember at one of our first meetings telling J. that I felt like smoking pot and that if I ever relapsed I wouldn't confine it to just alcohol. I definitely needed to immerse myself in the Steps.

Then, shortly into our sponsorship, I began developing feelings toward J. I understand why old-timers suggest that women sponsor women and men sponsor men. Needless to say, I was not prepared to be in a situation where I had to question my motives when it came to my own sponsor. I decided I needed to be honest with her.

In her wisdom, she made it very clear that she could no longer be my sponsor. I felt like I was in a whirlwind and my life as I knew it was done. I was suffering under the lash of my alcoholism and I was attracted to a woman. Not just any woman—my sponsor! God had a terrible sense of humor. However, some of the pieces of my puzzle were starting to fit.

J. urged me to start going to some LGBT meetings downtown. I thought I needed to play it cool so that maybe they would think I'd been out for a long time. It was like going to an AA meeting hoping no one would think I was an alcoholic. The funniest thing happened. I started hearing parts of my story: how I drank, how I felt. A few members even shared about coming out later in life. I met C.K. and asked her to sponsor me. And guess what? Her story is very similar to mine. I'd been in AA long enough to know I should stick around to hear the similarities. I clung to her like glue.

I was in such virgin territory. I knew nothing of what it was to show up as me, insecurities and all. I actually felt embarrassed because for the first time I couldn't fake it. I was a deer in the headlights. It took me a while to feel comfortable being out in gay AA.

I altered my appearance with a few piercings because that was what I was comfortable with. Holes could always grow back. I was somewhat into the shock value, but that was short-lived. All those aspects of myself that I'd been hiding because they weren't acceptable came bursting out of me in a somewhat comical fashion. I was a rebellious teenager trapped in a 30-year-old body. I knew I was home, and for the first time I could come clean with the secret I'd been hiding my entire life.

Peeling the layers off tested my sobriety in ways I couldn't have imagined. One of the biggest things was that I didn't know how to relate to my home group as a newly out lesbian. I made the decision to leave my group for almost a year.

C.K. had a gentle way of leading me through this often painful process. I'd grown up in a family where queers were made fun of and I'd adopted some homophobia that I seriously needed to look at. My prejudice was toward myself and how I believed God saw me: God didn't love me. He was just waiting for me to screw up, to say I told you so, and then I would get the punishment I deserved. That's the kind of Higher Power I came to Alcoholics Anonymous with. I would rather risk a life without a God than to have one that rejected me, so I rebelled at the idea of opening myself up to a Higher Power.

It took a long time to really trust that a Higher Power loves me and has my best interest at heart. It happened as I made my way through the Twelve Steps. When I decided to be fearless and thorough, withholding nothing, I became a useful and productive participant in my life.

Nothing could have prepared me for this sober journey. Every time I think I have an idea as to what my Higher Power has planned, I realize my plans are subject to change. I had an amends to make to my first sponsor. I was incapable of being completely honest with her when I decided to change sponsors. I came clean and shared my truth, and she couldn't have been any more encouraging and supportive.

I decided the only way I would truly be comfortable in my skin was to share my story at my old home group. After doing so, the women in the meeting came up to me and thanked me for sharing. I felt at home once again.

M. F.

CHAPTER 3

HOME AT LAST

Voices of gay male AAs

Will I fit in? That is the burning question many alcoholic gay men ask when they get to AA. Some find help for their alcoholism in special interest groups, others in mainstream AA, and most in a combination of both.

One writer says he found a group for LGBT AAs after several years of trying to stay sober in mainstream AA. "My struggle with my sexuality ... was one form of uniqueness that I felt justified my continuing slips," Larry T. writes. At the Lambda group that he joined, he saw other gay alcoholics staying sober and leading happy lives without self-pity. "My last excuse was gone. I was home at last!"

Another writer says he tried to be difficult when he called the AA hotline for help. "I said I needed to go to a gay meeting. I was thinking that maybe there weren't any and I could go on drinking. The woman said there were four that day in my area."

The alcoholics in this chapter have found that, yes, they did fit into AA, and are now able to pass on the support, love, and no-nonsense guidance of the Steps that changed their lives.

At Home in AA

NOVEMBER 1992 *(From Dear Grapevine)*

When I got sober, I wondered whether as a gay man I could fit into AA. I brought with me many self-centered fears about what others would think "if they only knew." Overall, however, my experiences have been positive, and I now feel more comfortable being open and honest about myself in AA than in the "outside world."

One particular event helped me. I traveled to Fresno, California, for some service work. Some people there knew I was gay, while others did not. I asked for a local meeting schedule—wanting a gay meeting, but afraid to be honest about that. When one of the men in the group gave me the schedule, he said, "Someone told me you were gay, so I underlined some gay meetings for you. A couple of guys from my home group told me these are good meetings."

I was touched by this gesture. It helped me to understand that I can share in the experience of seeing a fellowship grow up around me in AA, whether I am gay or straight.

B. C.
San Francisco, California

The Topic Is Change

FEBRUARY 2001

My home group is Lambda AA, here in Beaumont, Texas. In 1984, the founders of our group chose the eleventh letter of the Greek alphabet because it is the symbol of freedom for gays and lesbians. However, while most of our members are gay or lesbian, we welcome everyone. The only requirement for membership is a desire to stop drinking.

Some of our members have many years of sobriety, while others are brand new. But in keeping with the principle "One day at a time," we are fond of noting that whomever got up first that day has the most sobriety.

Over the years, we have had many memorable meetings. Three stand out in my memory. When I was new to the program, a young man in the last stages of AIDS celebrated his first sobriety birthday. He spoke of his battle to give up alcohol and drugs and of the many blessings God had bestowed upon him. His gratitude was manifest, despite the ravages of his disease. AA had given him more than sobriety; it had given him acceptance. It had given him serenity. It was a privilege to be there that night.

Several years ago, another member suffered serious health problems. When she got out of the hospital, she was unable to leave her apartment. So we brought the meeting to her. We crowded into her living room. She was propped up on a sofa and was very weak. When the chairperson asked if anyone had a topic, she spoke up from the corner and suggested "gratitude." It was a marvelous meeting and provided me with much-needed perspective. We continued to converge on her apartment for a meeting once a week or so, and after a few months, celebrated her thirty-fifth AA birthday with her. As she spoke that night, I realized that she had been working her program throughout her illness. This took courage, but it also took a good program. Imagine our joy as her health returned for a while, and she was able to rejoin us.

Then there was our group's tenth anniversary meeting, a Lambda Birthday. We were able to rent a large room from a local charity and the city, and thirty-four gay men and lesbians came for a great meal and a candlelight meeting. Among those present were several of our group's founders, still sober after many years.

Nevertheless, in the last two years, we have confronted a serious problem: declining attendance. This was a problem for us because we are a small group. We held numerous group consciences to discuss this. We tried Big Book studies, "Twelve and Twelve" studies, videos, and speaker meetings. Nothing helped.

As we went through the process of a group inventory, we gradually realized there were two issues: first, we needed to change meeting places; and second, each of us needed to reach out more to other suffering alcoholics.

Change or some version of it became a frequent topic at meetings. We all came to realize that change was healthy and needed, although I have to admit throughout this, I behaved like the alcoholic I was, am, and forever will be. Until matters reached a desperate stage, I was unwilling to consider any change. I was the same way when I was drinking: I was not going to change even though it was apparent to all but me that serious changes were long overdue.

Finally, we all let go and let God. Last night, we held our first meeting in our beautiful new quarters. Two of our group celebrated birthdays and sixteen of us were present. Sixteen is a crowd for us.

Our old (and beloved by me) meeting place was only part of the problem. We were the rest. I can speak only for myself, but I had ceased attending other meetings and went only to Lambda. I had largely stopped reaching out to newcomers and others in the program. My complacency was overwhelming. It is a tribute to the cunning, baffling, and powerful nature of alcoholism that throughout this time, I thought I was working a good program. It took only a few meetings at other groups for me to grasp how dangerous my complacency was to my sobriety. I am grateful that God gently reminded me of the Twelfth Step.

As I write, I do not know whether Lambda AA will survive. That is in God's hands, not mine. I am going to do my part by attending Lambda and other meetings, by sponsoring, by giving my phone number to newcomers, by going out for coffee instead of rushing home to watch ESPN. In short, I am going to try working all Twelve Steps for a change.

Bob B.
Beaumont, Texas

The Third Eye
MARCH 1994

M y name is Larry T., and I'm an alcoholic. I am also many other things, including a member of the Ft. Worth Lambda AA Group. Three years ago I wouldn't have been able to say that to anyone, but by the grace of God and the acceptance I have found at my home group, I've been able to face the secret that was keeping me sick.

My sobriety date is July 10, 1991, but the first time I walked through the doors of an AA group was June 12, 1987. There were many sobriety dates between those two, but those are the only ones I remember: the first one, and, I pray God, the last one. My first four years in the program were characterized by an honest desire to stop drinking and a total inability to do so. During those years, I was attending meetings almost daily at an extremely loving and Big Book-based "straight" group. I tried my best to work the Steps and do what the old-timers suggested, but I was never able to string together more than four months, one day at a time. At thirty-five years of age, I still hadn't faced the truth that had contributed more than any other single thing toward my drinking: I am homosexual. Lacking the strength and courage that I have since seen other gay alcoholics exhibit, I was determined that this was the one secret that I would take to my grave. So I sat in meetings day after day and listened to other AAs unload about problems with wives and girlfriends and get some relief from their burdens, while I sat silently and felt more and more apart. I have since learned that the sexual orientation I think I was born with didn't matter to the overwhelming majority of my fellow AAs; they just wanted me to get the program and find the happiness that they had found. But I was too damaged when I got here to risk sharing the truth about myself.

Please don't misunderstand: I believe that anyone, despite race, educational or economic background, sexual orientation or any other factor, can recover from alcoholism in any group in the world that adheres to the Twelve Steps as outlined in the Big Book of Alcoholics Anonymous. I also know that gaining that recovery depends absolutely on facing the truth about who and what we are, and that I was unable to do so in the group that I attended when I first found AA.

What finally made the difference when I discovered the Lambda Group was not any special magic I found there. It was what was taken from me: the last excuse I had for drinking. My life had become such a drunken nightmare of despair that I had run out of all other excuses, but I could always fall back on the old standby that the other people in my first group didn't understand—couldn't understand—what I was going through in my struggle with my sexuality. This was one form of uniqueness that I felt justified my continuing slips. When I got to Lambda, I saw something that I had never seen before—other gay alcoholics who were staying sober and leading happy and productive lives devoid of the self-loathing and self-pity I had wallowed in for so many years. My last excuse was gone. I was home at last!

Recently, I realized that, like most alcoholics, I had always felt somehow different from the people around me. It was as though I had been born with a third eye in the middle of my forehead. I could comb my hair down and cover it up and pretend to be like everyone else, but I always knew that my third eye was there, and that it made me different. When I walked nervously into my first AA meeting, I was thrilled to find a roomful of people with third eyes in the middle of their foreheads, just like me. But after the fog had lifted and a little reality set in, I began to notice that everyone else in the group had brown third eyes while mine was blue. I was still apart. Then, I found the Lambda Group and, for the first time in my life, found other people with blue eyes. And those eyes were clear and bright and happy to see me!

I am overjoyed to report that, if God as I understand him sees fit to keep me sober for three more days, I will have two years of continuous sobriety. My life is rich and full in ways that I could not have imagined during the black despair of my drinking days. My profession, my health, my family and so much more have been returned to me, and I have experienced a joyous freedom that I never dreamed could be mine. This was all made possible by a willingness to follow the Twelve Steps of Alcoholics Anonymous, not by the Ft. Worth Lambda Group. But it was the acceptance and understanding that I found there that allowed me to face the truth about myself, and so to begin recovery at last.

Alcoholics, probably more than most people, have a need to fit in and feel a part of things. Special interest groups can fill that need. If even one alcoholic can find the road to recovery in a special interest group, then such a group is justified. I am one alcoholic who did, and I'm eternally grateful for having had the opportunity for a new life that my particular special interest group afforded me. Indeed, I am sure that I owe my very life to having found Lambda, for it was there that I found AA, and it was in AA that I found God, and it has been through the grace of God that I have found a new way of living.

Larry T.
Hurst, Texas

Facing Fear

APRIL 2001 *(From Dear Grapevine)*

I just read the issue about diversity in our Fellowship (May 2000). Wow! I really identified. I'm a gay man who got sober in a city with a variety of meetings, including meetings for gay people. But I didn't realize until I moved to rural New Hampshire how much they meant to me. When I was first getting sober and full of anger and fear, they provided safe places where I could listen to the word of recovery and feel accepted for who I am.

Much of my work on acceptance and forgiveness had to start with self-acceptance. Now, a few years sober, I find I have more work to do. Almost without realizing it, I've let my fear of speaking out as a gay man in straight meetings near my hometown keep me away. After over two years in the area, I still haven't joined a single group in my area, and I travel fifty miles to my home group in Boston. Needless to say, my recovery has suffered.

Grapevine has helped me many times when I was in need—traveling for business, home alone, or just in need of a "meeting in print." But the May issue helped me understand how my own fear keeps me from getting healthier. And it made me see that if others react fearfully or negatively to me, it's their disease speaking, not mine.

Rob B.
Kensington, New Hampshire

Addressing the Wound
MAY 2008

When I was a little boy, I had two major nightmares: one was of a polar bear coming up the driveway and into the house to eat me, and the other was of a Tyrannosaurus rex looking in my window and then attacking me.

Both monsters were as scary as my dad. As a kid, he molested me and woke me up with beatings—tearing me out of bed, screaming and hitting—all while he was drunk. He would come home at three in the morning, drunk and mean, and terrorize me, calling me names and making me do household chores.

I hated him and he hated me. I became a sullen and rebellious child. I was never the son that he wanted. He wanted the all-American jock, but what he got was a brainy, nerdy, sissy-boy. I was an odd child, like a giraffe being raised by a family of deer.

To stuff my anger, to forget my feelings of aloneness, to cope with being "odd" (actually, I was gay but had no idea what was going on), I started stealing pills from my mom, smoking, overeating, and drinking whenever I could. The year I was sixteen, on Christmas Eve, while the family was at Midnight Mass, my best friend and I got drunk on creme de menthe and cola. I blacked out, broke a bottle of wine, and got blood everywhere. I urinated on the sofa. I was in heaven!

About a year later, I got into a fight with my dad while he was beating me, my mom, and my sisters. It was so violent that the police were called, and they escorted me off the premises. Me!

I was on my own. I drank whenever I wanted and used whatever I wanted. I managed to live that way for fifteen years. By age thirty-two, I was homeless, sleeping on my sister's sofa, and planning my suicide. At the time, I was only drinking two drinks a night—they were 20 oz. tumblers of gin on the rocks with no mixer, but I only had two, so I wasn't an alcoholic like my dad. But instead of killing myself that night, I went to bed with the idea that I would go through with it the next day if things weren't better.

The next morning, a thought crossed my mind: I'm an alcoholic. I need to go to AA. So I called the AA phone number in my area, and told them I wanted to go to a meeting. I decided to be difficult, and said I needed to go to a gay meeting. I was thinking that maybe there weren't any and I could go on drinking. The woman said there were four that day in my area. I couldn't stump her, so I took the information and went. I stayed sober that day, and the day after the meeting, and I'm still sober, nineteen years later.

About nine months into my sobriety, I was doing the Fourth Step and I wrote down every bad thing that my dad had ever done to me. My sponsor had the nerve to tell me to go through the list and write down my part in every one of those instances. My initial response to most everything my sponsor suggested was "Hell, no!" Then I would think about what she had asked me to do, talk myself into giving her suggestions a try, and darn if those suggestions didn't turn out to be the exact thing I needed to do.

I went through the list. He hit me … after I smart-mouthed him. He woke me up in the middle of the night, beat me, and made me water the front yard … after he had asked me to water it and I'd spent the day playing with my friends instead. He slapped me … after I'd said no in a mocking tone of voice. It was not a fun inventory.

Did he do horrible things that I had no part in causing? Yes. Was he mean and hateful and violent? Yes. Did he hurt and scar me? Yes. Can I change any of this? No. Was I difficult and rebellious? Yes. Was I lazy and self-centered? Yes. Did I steal from him? Yes. Can I change any of this? Yes.

At the time, he lived about fifteen miles away from me, but there was no way I could have gone there and had a conversation about this stuff without creating more resentment. Also, I could never have expressed my thoughts clearly, because anger and fear would have stopped me from saying everything I needed to say. So I wrote an amends letter.

He called me after he received the letter, and we spoke for about a half hour on the phone. In my entire life (thirty-four years at that point) my dad never said anything to me on the phone except, "Let me get your mother." So talking for half an hour was unheralded, truly overwhelming, and deeply moving for me. He forgave me for all I had done. He accepted my amends and agreed to my modest repayment plan for the money I had stolen from him. Then he said I was right—that things weren't good when we were younger and he drank too much. He didn't remember a lot of what happened, but said he was sorry for hurting me. He let me know he loved me. He cried and I cried.

I wish I could say we became best friends, but we didn't. We never had a close relationship—I never trusted him not to hurt me. He was human. Several times after the amends conversation, he said and did hurtful and hateful things. But we were changed men. We were never the same enemies again. We were family.

Four years ago, I was with him and my mother on the morning he died. I held his hand, and promised to help care for my mother so he could go peacefully. Mom lives with me now, as I promised.

Working the Steps and cleaning up my side of the street helped me. Although I could never forget the terrible things that happened, I could stop reliving them. I was able to stop tearing open old wounds with my resentments and hate. I can move on with a new life. I am at peace today with all that happened. Forgiveness has healed my soul.

Anonymous

In Defense of Special Groups

OCTOBER 1982 *(Excerpt from Dear Grapevine)*

I came into AA in 1971 and came out of the closet in 1976. All those first years were spent attending straight AA meetings. There was no gay AA in Portland and little in other towns. In 1976 in Vancouver, British Columbia, I went to my second gay AA meeting, and for the first time in my life (at fifty-one), I told a group of people that I was gay.

Soon after, Portland had a gay group, and I joined it. I did need the gay groups. Because of finally getting honest, I soon lost the stomachaches I'd had for thirty years. Also, I could finally work the Fourth Step.

I do not hide in AA anymore. If the need arises, I will say I am gay at a regular AA meeting. Our gay groups in Portland are all open to *all* alcoholics.

H. W.
Portland, Oregon

In the Center of Sorrow

FEBRUARY 2007

Two weeks before Christmas at my home group, I raised my hand and said that I was celebrating seventeen years without a drink. I gave credit to my Higher Power, the group, my sponsor, the program, meetings, and my willingness to put in the work. Each part was important in making it happen, I said.

That evening, my other half and I went to a holiday gathering. We sat in front of a warm fireplace and shared fellowship with friends. It was a perfect ending to the day. I went to sleep sober with a smile on my face and a grateful heart.

After saving for many years, we had bought our dream home and had an appointment to sign the final papers in two days. Uprooting our lives and packing for the move had been stressful, but still, things couldn't get much better.

Unfortunately, they got worse, much worse.

When I woke up the next morning, I took my usual few minutes to think about the day ahead. It was our last day in the old house, and there was last-minute packing to finish. I passed through the living room on my way to the kitchen to make coffee and saw my partner asleep in his chair—not an uncommon sight.

When I tried to wake him, I realized he wasn't breathing. I called 9-1-1, started cardiopulmonary resuscitation, and wanted to get drunk more than I ever had during my seventeen years of sobriety. This couldn't be happening, I thought. Deny it, it's not happening. Drunk. Get drunk. This isn't fair.

My heart ripped into pieces. I continued CPR as the 9-1-1 operator talked me through the procedure. The paramedics arrived and, within moments, the three of them were working on him like a six-handed lifesaving machine. Instead of looking for a bottle, I called a friend from my home group, told him what had happened, and asked him to meet me at the hospital. I was a mess and unable to drive; a deputy sheriff took me to the hospital.

My friend sat with me in the waiting area. When the nurse came, I saw in her eyes that the news was not good. They couldn't save him. My world crashed.

If the desire to be drunk had been strong before, it was nothing compared to what followed. Thankfully, I was not alone. My friend offered all the support he could as we started paperwork, made phone calls, and contacted my partner's out-of-town family. More program friends met us at my house. The phone rang and the doorbell chimed constantly in endless songs of support. A neighbor, also a sober member of AA, and his wife brought plates of food to feed the growing crowd. There was nothing anyone could do to make it better for me, but they kept me from picking up a drink and making it worse.

I was beyond consolation and in a fog the first few days, unable to see past the pain. My AA friends told me when to eat, when to sleep, and when to go to a meeting. They reluctantly respected my wish to be alone for a few hours at night when I tried to sleep.

As long as I do my part, I know I will get through this, even though I want to stay home to grieve and cry. I want to isolate and not show anyone my "weaker" side. But I go to my regular meetings, even if I don't want to. Each day, I call at least three people in Alcoholics Anonymous, even if I don't want to. It hurts, but I practice the Steps around my grief, fear, guilt, and loneliness, even though I don't want to. I relive the pain and write it down, even though I don't want to.

When I went to my first AA meeting more than seventeen years ago, members said I didn't have to drink, even if I wanted to. Now, to keep my part of the bargain, I do what the program has taught me to do, even if I don't want to.

I came into AA alone. Even with a handful of drinking buddies, I was still alone. Seventeen years later, with less than twenty-four hours notice by word-of-mouth, more than 200 sober members of AA came to the memorial visitation for my partner. The Fellowship made a big impression on his family. The message that AA carried showed how much he was loved and respected, and it was a priceless gift. Two weeks after the service, his mother called and asked for the address of the "friend of Bill" whom everyone talked about. The group's show of support touched his family and gave them more comfort than words ever could.

When my partner and I first moved to this area many years ago, we were the first open same-sex couple at local meetings. We learned later that some people wouldn't come to meetings that he and I attended. We showed up anyway because, as recovering alcoholics, meetings were a vital part of our sobriety. Ironically, some who had shunned us gave me the most support after his death.

I still have a huge gaping hole in my heart because my partner meant the world to me. I don't know how I can go on without him. But I keep putting one foot in front of the other, one day at a time. My experiences in most areas of my life have shown me that if I show up and do what's in front of me, I will be fine. I haven't had a problem yet that practicing the principles, Traditions, and Steps hasn't helped solve. I suspect that will hold true with my grief, fear, and loneliness, too. I just have to keep doing what I should, even if I don't want to.

Mark H.
Bartlett, Illinois

CHAPTER 4

FEELING DIFFERENT

Transgender, bisexual and other AAs discuss acceptance, uniqueness and alcoholism

So you think you're different ... that if you tell the truth, others will not accept you?

Most of these AAs had big secrets, like the AA member in this chapter, Tammy, who felt trapped in a male body yet was afraid to shed it and be herself. She had several slips, she writes, the last one a 36-hour binge. "I was sober a few days before I came back to my home group dressed as a woman and introduced myself as Tammy, an alcoholic and a transsexual. They were surprised, but supported me. I started my program the right way this time and have not had a drink since."

Being LGBT is not the only challenge these AAs struggle with. "At four and a half years sober, I was diagnosed with multiple personality disorder," writes one member. "AA was my bedrock."

Even though they felt different, when they allowed themselves to express who they were, they came to realize they're just alcoholics.

Welcome to the Big Top
APRIL 2004

In AA, we submerge our differences to focus on alcoholism as our primary problem. But this doesn't dismiss the notion that we come from widely divergent backgrounds. Recovery seems to work best when it is culturally relevant. Cultural relevance is just a fancy term for identification.

Some years ago, I received a call from a friend who was concerned because a man dressed in womens' clothing was attending meetings of her womens' AA group. Upon further inquiry, it became clear that he was an alcoholic, pre-operative male-to-female transsexual trying to find a place in AA to fit in. He just didn't feel comfortable in general AA meetings, mens' meetings, or gay/lesbian meetings. My friend's group was flexible, and the women there had big, warm, accepting hearts. So they took him in.

About a year ago, a friend and I were twelfth-stepping a new man in a restaurant. In addition to being an alcoholic, the man had been an intravenous drug user and a prison gang member. He was also on parole and his ethnicity was different from mine and my friend's. We were getting nowhere, so my friend called another member of our group. In addition to being an alcoholic, he also had been an intravenous drug user and a prison gang member. He was on parole, of the same ethnicity as the new man, and sober two years. He came over, and the two of them got along famously.

In both these instances—and many others—AA members operated in the finest tradition of Twelfth-Step work, meeting newcomers where they were at, not where we thought they ought to be; helping them identify; introducing them to other AA members with whose stories they might identify.

A few years ago, I met a new AA member who was an undercover narcotics detective. His job was to hang around bars and buy as many drugs as he could. (My old thinking said it sounded like a dream job!) But it was tough for him to stay sober under those circumstances. He didn't talk about his job at meetings, and he wasn't ready to let his fellow officers know he was in AA. So I encouraged him to attend an AA meeting for cops. He found this very helpful in maintaining his sobriety.

Another time, I met with an attorney who had written a textbook that was being used in law schools. Of course, that didn't keep him from getting thrown in jail when he got drunk and assaulted somebody. He was a bit pompous and quite impressed with himself. So he was thrilled when I asked him if he wanted to go to an AA meeting for lawyers. His colleagues cut him down to size pretty quickly, and they also started running him around to other AA meetings and introducing him to the Fellowship as a whole.

I've done similar things with doctors, priests, and pilots. As Bill W. wrote in Concept Twelve: "When our actors and cops and priests want their own private groups, we say, 'Fine! Why don't you try that idea out?'" These folks are sometimes over-identified with their professional roles, or their alcoholic behavior has threatened their ability to practice. Often they are excessively concerned that their patients, clients, licensing boards, or professional organizations will find out about their alcoholism. For those whose professional circumstances initially seem to pose a barrier to joining AA, these specialized AA meetings serve as a safe bridge into the wider world of Alcoholics Anonymous as most of us know it.

Of course, I know many professionals who do not attend profession-specific AA meetings. They simply don't find such meetings necessary or helpful in maintaining their sobriety. To each his own or, as we say in AA, *Live and Let Live.*

When I was active in young peoples' groups, I received a phone call from an old-timer complaining that young peoples' groups were trying to be separate and different and weren't really a part of AA after all. I was surprised, because I always thought that young peoples' groups were simply trying to present AA's message of recovery more effectively to young alcoholics. She just would not hear it and continued to berate the young peoples' movement. Finally I said, "Perhaps you're right. Why don't you talk it over at the closed womens' AA meeting you have at your house that I can't attend?" She got the point rather quickly after that.

To me, the International Conference of Young People in AA, the International Advisory Council for Homosexual Men and Women in AA, International Doctors in AA, International Lawyers in AA, and Birds of a Feather (for pilots) are all part of Alcoholics Anonymous. They may not be part of our general service structure, but they are part of AA. By action of the General Service Conference, these special international contacts are listed in the front of AA directories furnished by the General Service Office.

Our Fourth Tradition of autonomy ensures that we avoid the rigidity that would destroy AA and interfere with our ability to appeal to more and different kinds of sick alcoholics. We don't know how AA's message of recovery might need to be played out a century from now. But the AA groups of that time will know, and they will exercise their autonomy to meet that need.

Fortunately, we don't have formats and charters and regulations one must follow to start an AA group or hold an AA meeting. We have a body of experience, and we'll share it with anyone if they're interested. But if they want to try something new, we welcome that and actively encourage it. We don't just begrudgingly accept it. Every group has the right to be wrong—and often they turn out to be right.

When our co-founder Bill W. was newly sober, he was helped a great deal by reading *The Varieties of Religious Experience* by William James. Significantly, it wasn't called *The Similarities of Religious Experience*. There are many paths to the Higher Power. In AA, what's different is good.

We need more and different kinds of AA groups and meetings to appeal to the increasingly diverse alcoholics who come to AA today.

The Fourth Tradition's spirit of autonomy creates an atmosphere that allows this to happen. AA is a big tent, and there's room for all of us under the big top. And isn't the circus fun?

Paul C.
Oceanside, California

Double Trouble
MARCH 2005

When I was a child, I was really two people: Tom was the boy society accepted, and Tammy was the girl that society, especially the religious ones, condemned. You see, I am a transsexual, born with the body of one sex and the mind of the other. Rather than facing this dilemma, I conformed. Outside, I played and did "boy things," and at home, in my own space, I played with my Barbie and wore girl's clothes. I lived in constant fear of being found out. Most girls like me take the role of the opposite to the extreme, so it is not surprising that I joined a street gang and did many bad things to prove myself. It was hard to play this role, until I discovered alcohol after an eighth-grade graduation party. With alcohol, it was easy. Drinking became the solution for me from that first experience.

In high school, I had jobs and I kept up my grades. On weekends, when I was not working or studying, I hung out with the wrong crowd and got drunk every time I drank. Blackouts became a regular thing for me. I started acting like my favorite characters from movies I had seen, like *Easy Rider* or *Hell's Angels*. When I got my driver's license, I had the freedom to go places where I could dress as a girl. In the gay areas of Chicago, I could be myself. That's when my double life began to go into full swing. I tried three times to "purge" myself of the womens' clothes. That didn't work. I also started waking up in strange places with strange people. My drinking was getting worse.

One night in the late seventies, I was at a bar in Chicago. I was Tammy that evening. I watched the drag show and then left to go to my car, when I was arrested by Chicago vice for being in drag. They came up with a false charge of prostitution and booked me. I felt that life was hopeless and that I could never be myself. After that, my other self and drinking took over. The charges were dropped and my parents never found out.

I bought a Harley and became "The Wild One." I did forty states on that bike. When I stopped for the night and set up camp, I always made sure that I was in walking distance of a bar or other source of alcohol. I did not want to get a drunk driving citation, although I did get one later in my drinking career.

I always found jobs that enabled me to drink, so I never lost a job due to drinking until 1988. That day, sitting in a bar, I decided to go to college and become an accountant. I went back to school and drank a lot. I did manage to get a BA, but the alcohol affected my grades, and I graduated with a 2.99 average.

Still looking for work and hoping to have my own business and be my real self by the time I turned thirty-three, I settled for a job as a boss in a seal coating place. I worked for seven months, then went on unemployment for five months, all the time drinking and dreaming about my future.

The drinking continued and so did the endless supply of sexual partners. When I wound up sick in the hospital, it was discovered that I had AIDS and an enlarged liver. A caseworker came to my bed because I had no insurance at the time, and gave me information about a support group on the north side of Chicago. I attended the group, where I met a nurse who had about thirty years of sobriety. She "tricked" me into going to an AA meeting by suggesting another support group. It was a mostly gay HIV/AIDS AA meeting. At first, I did not admit that I was an alcoholic. They were so kind to me. After hearing all their stories, I came to realize that I was just like them—an alcoholic. However, I still was trying to hide my sexual identity. I even hit on this one girl who turned out to be a transsexual. Charlene told me to be true to myself. I didn't listen. I kept my secret and I stayed sober for only four months.

I drank, dressed up as Tammy, and went out to celebrate Market Days. The problem was that terrible combination of a head full of AA and a belly full of alcohol, and running into some of the "AA police." Thanks to all that, I stayed out only thirty-six hours. I was sober a few days before I came back to my home group dressed as a woman and introduced myself as Tammy, an alcoholic and a transsexual. They were surprised, but supported me. I started my program the right way this time and have not had a drink since July 1994.

Sobriety has not always been happy. One of my best friends, a roommate and a girl like me, died of this disease. I did not have to drink over that. My place in Chicago got flooded when a crank head set a garbage can on fire and the water flooded my apartment. But I did not have to drink over that. I have had major legal problems that landed me in the media, and I haven't had to drink over that. Last year, I lost my dad to cancer and felt the pain, but I reached out for help, not alcohol.

A few years ago God put a person just like me in my life. She now lives in Thailand. Because of my AIDS, I thought that I would never be able to get the operation to become the real woman that I dreamed about being my whole life. My friend knew of a doctor in Thailand who would do the operation. My parents sent me to Thailand and paid for the operation. After the operation, any cravings to drink were absolutely removed. I still continue to attend meetings to remind myself what would happen if I ever drink.

Today, I am happy and true to myself and I thank my Higher Power, the AA Fellowship, and my parents. I have grown through unity, service, and the love of AA, and hope that others like me can find what I have found. I am grateful that my dad knew he really had a daughter all this time and got to know her before he passed. So, if this drunk, biker, badass fake can become this beautiful woman inside and out, maybe others can also have hope.

Tammy W.
Kihei, Hawaii

Firm Bedrock
MAY 1999

In the Big Book, the section on sex comes right after the section on fear. It took me a long time to see how fear and sex were woven together in my life.

When I first got sober, the Big Book's idea about taking inventory about sex seemed simple enough. You put each relationship to the test: was it selfish or not? Gradually, that question became more difficult to answer, as my life got further away from drinking and more information came into my awareness.

I began to realize that perhaps I had some grave emotional and mental disorders. This sex business was much more complicated than it seemed at first. I had been sexually abused by my father and others. I am a lesbian. Drinking and sex were connected from the beginning, and once I started my own drinking, I left a huge trail of sexual wreckage. I did tremendous harm to myself and others.

There came a point in my sobriety when all I could figure out about sex was to stop doing it completely. The only thing that I knew for sure about God's will for me was that God wanted me to stay sober. My sponsor set an example for me by making it very clear that our relationship was to be absolutely nonsexual. I imitated her when I became a sponsor, and those relationships taught me a tremendous amount about love without sex.

At four and a half years sober, I was diagnosed with multiple personality disorder. I began to learn about taking responsibility for my behavior in a much more complete way. I put Alcoholics Anonymous firmly at the base of my recovery, and it was the one thing that I could always fall back on. I prayed a lot. I had a lot of therapy. I felt consumed by the enormity of dealing with my past, my childhood, my feelings and imaginings, my bitterness and resentment. I felt sure that I could never have a normal intimate relationship, and I was filled with despair and anger.

AA was my bedrock. It was the only thing that I was sure of, the only thing that I knew was good for me. Members of my home group heard me talk week after week from the depths of despair. I showed up at meetings no matter what, and held onto them for my life and my sanity. I kept it as simple as I could. The only value I could see in what I was going through was that I was truly able to be understanding and compassionate to others with similar backgrounds. I could empathize with their experience, and demonstrate that it was possible to stay sober.

I didn't drink, and an amazing thing happened. It all began to pass. The clouds lifted. Things cleared. I began sleeping through the night. I began to feel that I was healing. I had good days. I became interested in life again.

At nine years sober, I fell in love. I found myself in a relationship that meant the world to me. It was time to take a good look at sex and sobriety.

The line in the Big Book which has helped me the most is in the chapter "How It Works": "Whatever our ideal turns out to be, we must be willing to grow toward it." It took me a long time to begin to see what my ideal might turn out to be. Now that I have a pretty good idea of that, I work hard on my willingness to grow toward it.

I am blessed with a partner who loves me deeply. Although she cannot understand or relate to the terrors that I sometimes have around sex and intimacy, she is patient and loving and gives me the room to find myself, step by step.

I no longer pray to have my fear removed. Today, I pray that my love grows bigger than my fear, and that my humility becomes greater than my shame. On the days when I can say these prayers honestly, along with my daily prayer to do no harm, my sexual life is beyond my wildest dreams.

Recovery is possible, life is sweet, and drinking is the farthest thing from my mind.

Anonymous

Rigorous Honesty
JUNE 1982 *(From Dear Grapevine)*

How far should I go in being honest at AA meetings? This is a question that has been asked of me, and that I asked of my sponsor and other old-timers when I was new to AA. The answer was: "It is our secrets that kill us."

The problem for me is that I am homosexual. It also happens that I have been married and have children. In my first couple of years in AA, I was intimidated by members who insisted that I not speak of my gay partner, or that I avoid the discussion of relationships altogether. All the while, they had no hesitation in speaking of wives, husbands, mistresses, etc. My speaking of my lifestyle was considered in poor taste, and their affairs were considered comical.

After six years of sobriety, I find myself involved in AA more than ever before, and needing more involvement than I did as a newcomer. I am as honest as I am capable of being at meetings, and attend mostly regular AA meetings (and a few gay meetings). I have become less intimidated by close-minded people who would have me hide in the back of the room or just outside the door. My problems in life are the same as everyone else's—lack of self-esteem, difficulty with intimacy, yearning for a closer contact with God. To refuse to discuss my shortcomings, to keep that one secret inside, is choosing death over life, alcohol over sobriety.

I thank God for the willingness to make my life an open book more and more, and for the willingness to practice the principles of AA even though it may be difficult to do so at times.

J. B.
Tustin, California

Stand Fast
JUNE 2011 *(From Dear Grapevine)*

Recently, my new sponsor gave me an ultimatum after a meeting. "This is AA, not a drag show!" he said. "You've done everything but show yourself in a dress. This is not a game. Unless you can present yourself in a manner conducive to recovery, I can't work with you."

I had relocated from an urban area and had been working the Steps for over eight years. I'm not openly gay and didn't think I was that transparent. Perhaps he thought I could handle a little constructive criticism. But when I returned to the meeting hall, I had more shame, doubt, and uncertainty than I'd had at my first meeting.

AA has taught me rigorous honesty and to accept the things I cannot change. No one is going to sugarcoat this program. If someone calls you a sissy, keep coming back anyway. This disease is vicious. I refuse to become a victim or a statistic.

Anonymous
North Carolina

Whose Rules?

OCTOBER 2011 *(From Dear Grapevine)*

I read with dismay the letter "Stand Fast" in the June 2001 issue. The Third Tradition states: "The only requirement for A.A. membership is a desire to stop drinking." It says nothing about having to present ourselves in any particular fashion, especially not in a manner conducive to recovery. This is just a rule the writer's sponsor made up for himself (or got from someone else). Thank God that this isn't a fact for us all. I would never have made it thirteen years if someone had told me I had to behave, or dress, a certain way. My sponsor told me to go to meetings and not drink in-between, work the Steps, pray daily, and call her if I felt like drinking. Just that was a pretty tall order for me. More power to Anonymous for staying sober with someone laying non-AA "rules" on him.

By the way, people I stay sober with sometimes go to meetings in drag, and many have been sober far longer than I. Gay people can, and do, stay sober.

Mike H.
Seattle, Washington

Above All, an Alcoholic

SEPTEMBER 1982

Scared out of my wits, sick, shaking, confused, lonely, I drove past that AA hall again and again, waiting until the last possible moment before I had to open that door. I had been at this point before and always had some "good" reason for backing out. This time, there were no reasons. All that was left at the ripe old age of twenty-five was the ruins of a young family.

But what was going to happen when I walked through that door? What were those people going to ask me? How could I tell them that I might have a drinking problem, that I didn't know what was happening in my life anymore, that I had squandered thousands of dollars, that I hurt people and hated myself, that I was married and had a little girl, and that I was gay? Oh God, they wouldn't understand. They'd look at me with utter disgust, incredulity, and righteous judgment in their eyes.

Pain is a great motivator. I got out of the car, took a few breaths, held my head up, and walked toward that door. "If it's too awful," I said to myself, "I can leave." I had become quite accustomed to rejection. "There are not a whole lot of people who *could* understand," I told myself. "So what's one more time? I don't know where else to go."

I opened the door and walked into the warmth, the laughter, the acceptance, and the love that is AA. No one asked me who I was or what I wanted; no one asked me how much money I had or what I did for a living; no one asked me where I did my drinking or what my sexual preferences were. The smiling man who greeted me told me that if I thought I had a drinking problem, I was in the right place. "Don't compare your story to the one you'll hear tonight," he suggested. "Try to *relate* to what he says, to what alcohol did to him as a human being."

Well, my Higher Power was apparently working overtime that night, because I did relate to the speaker. When he was finished, I knew I was an alcoholic, not a lunatic, not an evil, immoral wretch, but a sick person suffering from a disease of body, mind, and spirit and if I wanted to get well, AA could help. And it has.

The process of getting and staying sober has been far from easy. Years' worth of guilt, self-hatred, resentment, and fear don't go away overnight. It takes a lot of work, a lot of prayer. Above all, it requires physical sobriety. But believe me, it does get better.

The first year I was sober, nearly all my energy went into AA:

meetings, meetings, meetings; getting as active as I could; reading and studying the Big Book and *Twelve Steps and Twelve Traditions*; visiting institutions and rehab centers; talking with new
people about the program; going along on Twelfth Step calls and
to AA conferences and social gatherings; and slowly, ever so slowly opening up to these people, whom I found I could trust.

Time passed quickly, and I discovered one day (with the help
of an old-timer) that I, too, had learned how to stay sober. He
told me that I looked healthy, had a genuine smile now, and had
that "AA look" in my eyes. I was made aware that my ballooned
ego was being replaced with self-respect, that resentment and
hatred were being replaced with tolerance and understanding,
that fear was being replaced with trust, and that loneliness and
self-pity were being replaced with gratitude and love—all because I was working the program to the best of my ability and
wasn't drinking.

I kept coming back as I was told, for there was—and still is—
much work to do. When the time arrived for me to deal with what
I thought was the most hideous aspect of my character, I was able
to. With the help of a Higher Power and the people in AA, I made
it and am making it, sometimes tearfully but more often joyfully.
When I entered AA, two and one-half years ago, there were no gay
groups in our area. I didn't know where to turn. Slowly, as I became ready, God put people in my life—some gay, some not, some
new people, some old-timers. We have stayed sober and grown
together. By applying the principles and program of AA, I have
gained my freedom—freedom to be myself, to like myself as I am,
to become whatever it is that my Higher Power has planned for
me, one day at a time—freedom to live the type of life I'm most
comfortable with, to love, and to laugh.

If there is one slogan in the program that is more important
than another to me, it is "First Things First." Above all else, I must
remember that I am an alcoholic, that I must remain willing to
go to any length to maintain my sobriety, or I will die. Gay or

straight, black or white, Jew or Christian, rich or poor, it won't make a bit of difference if I choose to drink. For with me, as with every alcoholic, to drink is to die.

J. B.
Toledo, Ohio

A Minority of One
OCTOBER 1997

By the time I crawled through the doors of Alcoholics Anonymous, I felt like a minority of one. In fact, I had pretty much always felt that way. I was the first child of a loving family with an extended kin network, so where did all of that fear, doubt, and insecurity come from? How did the pretty little girl who made all As and sang in the church choir end up as the only woman drunk on a street corner with the guys? Whatever caused it, it was not that I am an African-American or that I am a lesbian.

When I started to drink at age fifteen or sixteen, I drank like an alcoholic. This made me a minority right away since my peers in high school were not particularly interested in booze. It was the sixties, and shortly after I became a teenaged drunk, I gravitated toward as many of the movements of that era as I could, becoming a black militant hippie peacenik gay activist drunk. All the while I was glorying in my uniqueness. I disputed even those who seemed to understand me because I really needed to be one of a kind: I thought it was all I had.

In 1977, at the age of twenty-seven, I finally made it to Alcoholics Anonymous. I'd been to quite a few meetings before that in treatment centers, detoxes, and court-ordered circumstances. But it wasn't until 1977, when I ended up with a bottle on a street corner, that it hit me like a hammer that I was at the end of the line. I said a prayer—just a little one, but quite distinct, that came up from someplace deep inside me. It transformed a curse into a cry for help. When I came to, I was in a detox; and after that, I spent almost a year in a halfway house, getting sober. Around Easter 1978, I finally surrendered all the way, letting go of the marijuana and the prescribed "mood elevators," and I began to look for a Higher Power.

One of my sponsors used to tell me, when I was feeling especially put upon by members of my own species, "You've got to have people—that's all there is!" Vulnerable, hurt, and needy, I sincerely doubted this. But God started to show its face in a parade of people brought before me, usually just at the right time. My first sponsor in AA was the only other black woman AA in the area; we were kind of pushed together even though we didn't have much else in common. We did share alcoholism and the desire to stay sober, and that was enough. This woman told me to call her every day at 6 P.M. sharp, gave me a Big Book, and said, "Let's get started" and "Let's grow together."

The first person I sponsored in AA was a gay white man from the South; he was also several years younger than I was. His Higher Power whispered in his ear that I should chair a workshop at the annual gay and lesbian AA round-up on the experience of being a gay person who got sober at "straight" meetings; so he signed both of us up as co-chairs. That workshop was standing-room only.

My first partner in sobriety tried to show me how precious I was, just exactly the way I was at that moment. I wasn't ready for it at the time, but I remember the effort and the love with gratitude. Then, fearful and ashamed, when I was sober a little over three years, I went home to face my family, and they welcomed me with shining eyes, love and forgiveness, and lots of hugs.

Somewhere along the line, I'm not sure when, I came to believe that my experiences and who I am have been given to me for the express purpose of passing along a certain message, inside AA and outside of it. As it says in what many call the Promises—what I refer to as "the guarantees" since the book says that they will always materialize *if we work for them*—"No matter how far down the scale we have gone, we will see how our experience can benefit others." As one of my AA friends likes to say, "God is good."

Some days, I still feel like a minority of one. I go to meetings where it seems that everyone else is sober a few days or a few years, and where to some my double-digit sobriety makes me look like I have all the answers and don't have difficulties or need to make amends. Alcoholism still occasionally whispers from a small place inside me, planting fear, doubt, and insecurity if I do not exercise constant vigilance.

I recently moved back to what I sometimes call "the scene of the crime": the city where I was born and grew up. I feel very sure that I was brought back here for a specific purpose though I may not be given to know what it is. Perhaps it is to live my amends to my family and old friends, clean up my side of the street going back as far as the story goes. Walking through the doors of an AA meeting today, I feel at home, and love the sound of our many different voices coming together at the end of a meeting to pray the Lord's Prayer or the Serenity Prayer. I am grateful today that God's voice is stronger and surer than my occasional negative whispers, comforting me through difficult times, letting me know that I am part of the whole.

D. E. S.
St. Louis, Missouri

One Size Fits All
AUGUST 1982 *(From Dear Grapevine)*

At one time, I belonged to a minority. After all, I was unique. As it turns out, so many of us thought we were unique that we constitute a majority.

One of AA's great strengths seems to be its diversity—"a wrench

for every nut." But our program is really a single, adjustable tool—
"One size fits all"—that works because our similarities are so much
greater than our differences.

From the day I first walked through the doors of AA, I knew
that despite all appearances and my expectations, the only difference between me and the people at that meeting was that they were
sober, joyous, contented alcoholics and I was still suffering. Today,
the circumstances in my life can and do make me feel isolated and
different—when I let them. My circumstances may be different, but
they do not make me different. I am not a gay alcoholic or a black
alcoholic or a female alcoholic. I am just an alcoholic.

Anonymous
Glen Ellyn, Illinois

CHAPTER 5

ROOM FOR ALL OF US

Finding acceptance, love and guidance in the Fellowship

Although some LGBT members experience adversity in and out of AA, fellow recovering alcoholics show them how to use the Steps and Traditions to find a better way of life, a Fellowship, and a Higher Power. The sponsors and the home groups who didn't see a person's sexual orientation as an issue helped these members feel safe enough to stick around AA.

One AA in this chapter is not gay. Justin P. writes that he had prayed to get rid of resentment about homosexuality, but it wasn't lifted until he took the opportunity to sponsor a gay man. "I had the privilege of hearing this man's Fifth Step, and thus came to a greater level of understanding," he writes.

"Finally, with my back to the wall, I got a sponsor," K.K. writes. "I was accepted for exactly who I was: an alcoholic trying to get sober. My sexual preference had nothing to do with my sobriety."

With this trust established, these AAs moved forward in their recovery.

Quiet Guidance
MAY 1990

Whenever I hear sponsors mentioned in AA meetings, I think about the sponsors I've had since September 1974, when I first got to AA.

I remember my first sponsor. Let's call her Wilma, since that wasn't her name. I asked her to be my sponsor after my first AA meeting. Wilma was the only one who spoke to me before the meeting, and she spoke with great enthusiasm about AA and sobriety for some time during the meeting. Someone had said during the meeting that having a sponsor was very important. So I quickly asked Wilma to be my sponsor. I also picked her because she made me feel comfortable. We were very much alike in personality and attitudes. She even thought it was hip, slick, and cool that I was gay, even though she was definitely heterosexual.

But I stayed sober only about ninety days. I went to lots of AA meetings and had great enthusiasm about sobriety, but I don't remember working any Steps. I got drunk shortly before Christmas 1974. But about nine months of drinking was all I could take before crawling to the phone to send up a white flag of surrender. I still vividly remember the phone call I made to Wilma that September day when my ego had been squashed like a bug on a windshield and I was desperate to get back to AA.

But Wilma was drunk. She'd started drinking a few weeks after I did. After I found my own way back to AA, several people told me that Wilma had been in AA for a number of years but had never been able to stay sober for more than about a year. I waited almost six months this time before getting serious about picking another sponsor. And I read the Big Book and began working the Steps.

About the time I saw Step Four looming on the horizon—working the first three Steps daily had become automatic—I started searching for a sponsor. I talked after meetings and over coffee with some of the older members of the groups I was attending, and I still believe they gave me some good suggestions on how to go about finding a sponsor.

One fellow told me to only consider those who'd been sober for at least seven to eight years. This, he felt, was long enough for them to get over what he considered to be the silly and egotistical habit of summarizing their sobriety as a set of rigid rules which they then foisted upon their sponsees. "Remember," he said (in so many words), "thousands of drunks all over the world have gotten and stayed sober solely on the basis of the AA program as described in the AA books and discussed in meetings. But all you know about one person's special rules is that one person has stayed sober by following them."

Another person told me to watch out for people who reminded me too much of myself in terms of personality, attitudes, or outlook on life, because, if we were very much alike, we'd share the same blind spots. A third person suggested I consider someone who had something that I wanted for myself in my future sobriety—not someone who had what I already had. And someone else told me to check people out. "See if they walk like they talk," she said. "Check them out with some of the old-timers so you don't pick someone who's making habitual use of AA's swinging door," she added, knowing my earlier experience with Wilma.

Another woman in AA gave me some specifics. "When you find someone you think might fill the bill," she said, "get a phone number and use it. Do this with several people. Use them as if they were your sponsors by calling them when you have a problem or a question. Do this for a while and you'll find yourself eventually calling only the person who'll be a good sponsor for you. The others will drop by the wayside," she said. "They won't be home most of the time when you call, or they'll be too busy to talk to you when they are home. They'll want to do all the talking and won't be able to listen to you. Or you'll be afraid to talk to them about problems for some reason you may not be aware of until you try. The important thing," she continued, "is that you'll end up with the right person this way, even though you're not doing the picking. It'll feel to you like your sponsor is picking you. It's like what they say about co-incidences being the way God works best, and that God does his best work anonymously. Your sponsor will be picked for you in a way that seems like a coincidence, but it won't be," she said with a strange little smile that I didn't understand for years.

I followed many of these suggestions, the most difficult being to ask people for phone numbers and then call them. But I made myself do it, for the person who'd suggested I try potential sponsors out on the phone for a while had also said that if I couldn't do this now, I might not be able to do it later.

When I was about nine months sober, I picked as a sponsor a woman I never would have picked when I was newer. Thelma was very much unlike me. I was in my late twenties; Thelma was about sixty. I was definitely a lesbian; she was definitely not. I was a university graduate student; Thelma had made it through high school. She even wore all those bright and ill-fitting housedresses—clothes I would never be caught dead wearing.

I could tell right away that she wasn't bigoted against gays, for when I mentioned I was homosexual, she didn't bat an eye. She just looked at me as if I'd confessed to liking popcorn. And the look said better than any words could that my sexual orientation had nothing to do with AA, sobriety, or her as my sponsor.

In this and other ways, Thelma made me feel at home in AA, and I lost that feeling of being different. After a few months of having Thelma as my sponsor, I even lost the feeling I'd had most of my life that if people *really* knew me and all that I'd done in my life, they'd tell me to get lost. I became just another alcoholic in a room full of alcoholics. I remember what Thelma told me when I asked her to be my sponsor. She told me that she could be my sponsor as long as I remembered one important thing: she had clay feet. "Don't put me on a pedestal," she said. "If you do, I'll fall off."

Thelma had nothing especially new or insightful to say on how to stay sober or work the Steps. On sobriety, she said, "To stay sober, don't drink." Whenever I asked her about working the Steps, she just said, "Read the book. The directions are in it."

Thelma was definitely spiritual, the quality that had drawn me to her in the first place. But there wasn't a religious bone in her body. This proved fortunate for me, for I did not know it then but the sober years to come would show me I had some deep-rooted resentments against organized religion based on childhood experiences, including a parents' use of God as a punishing and vengeful deity.

It has taken years for these wounds to heal. During that time, all I could do to help the process was choose *not* to practice, a day at a time, the resentments that had grown like scabs on these childhood memories. This especially meant not getting caught up in similar resentments expressed by others in meetings.

Thelma told me about the Great Spirit of the universe, since she was half American Indian and found the Indian practices and beliefs more in keeping with her own spiritual experiences. She never lectured me about spirituality, but then Thelma never lectured me about anything.

Thelma always listened to me, no matter how long I needed to talk. If I was ranting on about some injustice I'd experienced, Thelma let me rattle on until I ran out of steam. Then she would tell me about an experience she'd had when she was certain that someone was treating her unjustly. The endings of such stories drawn from her experiences were always the same: "And then time passed, I got over my hurt, and later found out I had been wrong about that person." She'd find out that the person she'd thought was intentionally hurting her was doing no such thing or that the injustice she'd felt was no injustice after all.

I must have done a lot of ranting in those days, for I can remember hearing about a number of Thelma's experiences of this sort. At other times, when I had no problems and we were just talking,

Thelma would patiently tell me about how impossible it was to know the truth when anger locked me into my own point of view. But she usually phrased it as the need for "walking a few miles in the other person's moccasins."

In meetings, those who didn't know her probably thought of her as a quiet older woman who sat in the corner and listened carefully to everyone who spoke. From her example, reinforced by others I knew in those days, I learned how to quiet my mind and truly listen to others so that I could hear what I needed to hear that day.

One old-timer explained it this way to me: "Don't let your mind rattle on at meetings. Then all you'll hear from someone else is something that gets you thinking about what you have to say. Listen to everything the person talking has to say as if your life depended on it—because it might one day. Listen to everyone this way, especially the ones you want to ignore," this old-timer said. "God won't deprive you of the answer you need, if you've come to an AA meeting needing an answer. He may, however, have your answer come out of the mouth of the person you least expect to have your answer from. God has a sense of humor."

I never heard Thelma criticizing anyone other than herself. If she didn't agree with someone, she was silent or spoke about something else. And when I asked her a question, Thelma wasn't afraid to say, "I don't know. Let's ask someone else."

The most consistent policy in Thelma's approach to sponsorship was her refusal to give me advice about anything. If I phoned her about a problem, she would listen carefully, not interrupting even if I took five minutes to give every insignificant detail. After a moment of silence, Thelma would share with me one of her experiences. Sometimes the experiences weren't similar, but the feelings or reactions were the same. Thelma never used sharing experience as a roundabout way of telling me what to do, either. In talking about her experiences, she was vague about the details but very clear about her feelings and even clearer about what she had to consider before making a decision. She was much clearer about the process of making that decision than she was about exactly what decision she made.

It took me years to realize what Thelma was doing, not only teaching me how to make decisions on my own but also how to see the common thread running through human experiences so I could avoid getting sidetracked so easily by the details. Once she said something like this: "If I told you what to do, and it worked, you would have no one to thank but me. All you would learn to do is be dependent on me to do your thinking and deciding for you. Even though you want very much right now for me to tell you what to do, if I did this you would one day come to hate me for it, because one day you would resent it as a way I have kept you weak and powerless."

Thelma told me that, no matter how much I feared making bad decisions, I could not learn how to make good decisions except by making decisions. "You'll make mistakes," she said. "We all do. You will make some bad decisions before you learn how to make good ones. But what is true about good decisions is also true about bad ones: You will always learn from the consequences."

Thelma did not tell me to grow up. She allowed me to grow up. She gave me lots of elbowroom for growing, giving me no rules to follow (or break) regarding meetings to attend or required check-in phone calls or visits to her. As I grew, I began to learn as much from her methods as from what she said to me, especially in the years that followed when circumstances took me hundreds and then thousands of miles from Thelma.

Thelma was my sponsor. She was never my Higher Power.

I say was because Thelma has disappeared from the face of the earth. Some call this death. But what is important is that I haven't lost Thelma. I've just gained another invisible means of support.

Anonymous

Fitting In

DECEMBER 1988 *(From Dear Grapevine)*

This letter is in response to the letter in the September 1988 issue of Grapevine from Minneapolis, Minnesota requesting more gay material in the magazine.

In my opinion, Grapevine has a lot of useful articles about getting and staying sober within the Fellowship of AA. It discusses the Steps and Traditions in many different ways that help tremendously. When I told my sponsor I am a lesbian she said, "So what. You want to get sober don't you?" I'm the one who usually makes a big deal out of being gay. At times it can be like another ego.

The truth of the matter is I'm just like any other alcoholic who wants to stay away from a drink one day at a time and I do belong in a world of human beings where, as a drunk, I thought for sure I would never fit in. I do belong to a special interest group which helps me with situations dealing with my sexuality, or like everyone else, I talk to my sponsor and friends if my situation is a little too personal to share with a group of people. Today when I go to a meeting, any AA meeting, my primary purpose is to stay sober and help other alcoholics achieve sobriety. It doesn't matter whether they're black, white, Indian, straight, gay, or asexual, the program of Twelve Steps is designed for everyone. Being a lesbian is just part of who I am. When I'm looking for more attention because of this characteristic, I know I'm not joining the rest of the world. I do fit in.

B. H.
Asbury Park, New Jersey

Love and Tolerance

OCTOBER 2000 *(From Your Move — Responses from readers to the special section in the May 2000 Grapevine titled, "Is AA for Everyone?")*

Kudos on your piece, "Is AA for Everyone?" in the May issue. This is a topic that is worth exploring collectively and individually.

The first person who asked me to sponsor him in the program was a gay man. I had reservations about doing this, as I am not gay, and reacted with fear and ignorance. I called my sponsor to get his opinion on the right thing to do. Being the good sponsor that he is, he referred me to Traditions One, Three, Five, and especially Ten. I was reminded that I was to have no opinion on outside issues while acting in my capacity as an AA member.

I continued to work with this man, and thank God I did. I had the privilege of hearing this man's Fifth Step, and thus came to a greater level of understanding. Prior to this occasion, in my own Fifth Step, I'd discovered that I had a resentment against homosexuality. During my amends, I prayed for understanding and to have this resentment removed. It wasn't until I was able to work with this man that this was accomplished.

"Love and tolerance of others is our code" (*Alcoholics Anonymous*, p. 84). My Higher Power put this person in my life to teach me this wonderful concept and to give me the opportunity to make a living amends.

I've been sober the past six years and have done Twelfth Step work with a wide variety of people from many backgrounds. I know today that we are all truly perfect children of a loving God, however we choose to define him.

Personal sobriety is an important pursuit in AA, but no less so than the pursuit of our collective well-being. I'm glad I have had a sponsor who gives as much emphasis to the Traditions as to the personal program of recovery.

Justin P.
Missoula, Montana

The Only Requirement
MAY 1975

I'm an alcoholic. I'm twenty-seven. I'm a woman. I'm a homosexual. I've been sober in the beautiful Fellowship of AA for seventeen months and, for the first time in many years, find myself smiling, laughing, and really caring for other people.

After ten years of alcoholic drinking, that life of horror, loneliness, and despair brought me to the doors of my first AA meeting. In the first few months of my sobriety, I tried to follow suggestions, went to many meetings, joined a group, and found myself a sponsor whose sobriety I respected. But during this time, I lived in fear within—fear of my homosexuality being discovered, fear of being rejected by fellow AA members, fear of being left alone to cope with my disease of alcoholism. This fear drove me so close to the first drink that I believed I could never maintain the sobriety I so desperately needed and wanted. I became distrustful of my fellow AAs. My fears became my biggest problem, instead of my alcoholism.

Finally, I heard a speaker ask, "Are you willing to go to any lengths to maintain your sobriety?" Who would understand my situation? Whom could I trust? *Was* I willing to go to any lengths to stay sober?

In desperation, I went to my sponsor. I cried, sweated, and shook. But the words I hated to say came out, painfully and slowly. I sat back, waiting for a word or a look of rejection.

My sponsor simply smiled and told me that she was an alcoholic just like me and that this was how and why she could help me.

I thank my Higher Power every night for this program that saved my life—a program of "principles before personalities." "The only requirement for AA membership is a desire to stop drinking," our Third Tradition says, and there is a place for every person who wants help. There is a place for me. I thought that I was unique, different, that I had nowhere to turn in this world for help. But thanks to the program of AA, I have found the way to a full and happy life.

Anonymous
Rhode Island

No Boundaries, Please
JULY 1987 *(Excerpt from Your Move)*

When I first came to AA, I already felt like an outcast. All my life I had heard jokes about or had glimpsed fingers pointed at me for being homosexual. You know, "one of *those* people."

Now I was told to stop drinking, join a group, and get a sponsor. Wow, that was some tall order to fill. I managed to stop drinking and I joined a group, but get a sponsor? Who among my newfound friends would want me around?

Finally, with my back to the wall, I got a sponsor. Oh, I tested her and tested her, once more fearing rejection, before I finally said, "I'm gay." She kept right on sharing with me before I blurted it out again.

"So what?" she responded. She didn't throw me out of her home, nor did she run to meetings and say, "Guess what, here's another of those people."

I was accepted for exactly who I was: an alcoholic trying to get sober. My sexual preference had nothing to do with my sobriety.

K. K.
Patchogue, New York

The Rabbit Hole
AUGUST 2003

"It's all about spirit," my first sponsor used to say. "Either you're walking the path to know spirit better or you're not. AA is a spiritual program that will save your life—literally—as long as you walk the path." Working the Steps, I have realized that my spiritual journey started long before I ever entered AA.

As a child, I had the knowledge that there was much more going on than my five senses could pick up. I knew that I was on a "holo-deck" like the one in the popular sci-fi series on TV. If I could find the right button to push or the right command to say, the computer-generated environment would disappear and I would see all the beautiful spirits on the other side of the veil. My search for this button, or escape hatch, began when I was seven or eight years old.

It was an extremely frustrating search. My parents had no time for child's play, since it interfered with their drinking. My grandmother, however, saw my frustration and lovingly sent me out to look for the entryway behind trees and under rocks. After she read *Alice in Wonderland* to me, I knew, with all my being, that there was a rabbit hole to the other side for me. When she died, just before my ninth birthday, I was devastated. How could I search without her support?

My search became desperate. My mom and dad were drinking all the time. When they weren't passed out, they were fighting, and my father was very violent. Being threatened with loaded guns, axes, knives, and the possibility of being drowned were all too frequent. I needed to escape the insanity. Then one day, my dad let me finish his beer. The next day, I *asked* to finish his beer. Soon, I began stealing beer, and by the time I was eleven years old, I drank every weekend with my best friend. We raided our parents' bars and got smashed in the basement.

Once I became a teenager, I started drinking every day. As the violence at home intensified and I feared for my life on a daily basis, I drank to escape the major anxiety I was feeling. I still hadn't found the rabbit hole to the other side where it was safe and where my grandmother lived, and at some point during my teenage years, I gave up. I was so distraught that all I wanted to do was drown myself in alcohol.

My drinking progressed rapidly. I drank to escape. I drank to get drunk. There were no holds barred in my life. I went at one hundred and ten miles an hour over the edge every day. I did my best not to survive my life. I lived through multiple car accidents, major falls, and extremely dangerous stunts. I thought I was invincible. Alcohol built a tough shield around me. There was nothing coming in and nothing going out. I was a rock.

During the darkest time of my life, when I was nineteen or twenty years old, an angel entered my life. Diane was my college roommate. She didn't drink much, and she went to church. She was bubbly and full of life, and for some reason we clicked. She made me smile like no one ever had. She was kind and loving like my grandmother, and in spite of my drinking, she was always good to me. She loved me and I fell in love with her. I had never fallen in love with anyone before. I had been in relationships with boys since the second grade, but they were more a convenience than something meaningful. Diane was pure goodness. Her love cracked the shield that was around me. I couldn't believe all the feelings I was having: intense love for her, intense fear about possibly being gay, intense pain and shame from a lifetime of drinking. I was overwhelmed, to say the least. Then one day Diane came to me and said she was going to get married to a guy. I was lost beyond measure. It sent me to my bottom.

My heart was exposed for the first time, but I couldn't talk about my pain because then people would suspect I was gay. At the same time, I couldn't keep the pain in anymore because Diane had cracked my shield. I was living alone, drinking cases of beer daily and snorting cocaine to distract myself. I was tormented to the point of total desperation.

After praying for months to something I was not sure existed, I was heard. After a horrendous night of drinking and making a fool of myself, I realized life was no longer worth living. The next day, instead of getting up in my usual way, I went back to sleep, hoping to never wake up again. At 4:00 P.M., I woke up, knowing I could not drink anymore and where to get help—Alcoholics Anonymous. Also, the desire to drink had been lifted from me. The next day I called AA, and the man on the phone asked me to go to a meeting that night and told me where it was. It never occurred to me to do anything other than follow his suggestion.

I entered AA desperate and annihilated. I had no willpower to carry on and no desire to go back and slam my head against the wall for the thousandth time. I was beaten and I turned my life over to my sponsor and the fellowship of the program. I did what they told me to do—everything—and my life started to get better. I felt most relieved when I realized that these were the people who could help me find the rabbit hole I had always searched for. They called it "God as I understand him." It didn't matter to me what it was called. I now had permission and help to look for whatever it was.

My sponsor was Catholic and believed in Jesus, going to church, and praying on her knees. I believed in the trees and standing outside in a forest. Religion seemed too rigid for me. I couldn't imagine memorizing all the words one would have to say in church in response to a priest. Religion was not my path, so now what?

One day I found myself reading the book *Seth Speaks*, one of a series of books channeled by Jane Roberts. It blew my mind wide open because for the first time I'd read something that sang to my heart. This was the other world that I had always known existed, and Jane had access to it. I had found the rabbit hole! I could not read these books fast enough. I had an insatiable thirst to know Spirit. When a channeled book said that homosexuality was a sin or an abomination, I would discard it immediately and move on to the next. I knew I was not an evil person because I was gay. For my life lessons, my Spirit chose not only to be an alcoholic, but also a lesbian. I refused to let some human, let alone channeled entity, tell me that I was not perfect as I was.

As my desire to know Spirit grew, I read countless books in search of greater understanding. I discovered that the universal truths of the Twelve Steps are echoed everywhere in books dealing with spiritual growth. As an alcoholic, I am very fortunate that it is suggested that I work the Steps of the program. I am expected to work them if I want to get better, and through sharing with my sponsor and people at meetings, I have let go of all my secrets and have found serenity. It has been a very slow and uneventful process, without any much-desired lightning bolts. But today, I have a very strong and firm foundation in AA and a deep and loving connection with my higher self.

The true blessing I have discovered in AA is written in "How It Works": "May you find God now." With the love and support I have received from AA, I have discovered the rabbit hole. On November 28, 2002, Thanksgiving Day, I celebrated twenty years of sobriety. I know now that my grandmother is always with me; I am no longer separate from God. My sponsor was right—this is a spiritual program, and for this I am deeply grateful.

Heidi E.
Conway, Massachusetts

CHAPTER 6

LOVE AND TOLERANCE

*Dealing with judgment and lack of acceptance, these
AAs looked for answers*

The LGBT members in this chapter talk honestly about some of the things they've seen and heard in the rooms and at AA gatherings. Many of these members write about the importance of special interest groups and meetings, especially in early sobriety.

"Alcoholics Anonymous is probably the only organization in this community that is open to anyone who wishes to attend," writes Stephen S., from Minnesota. "AA's policy of tolerance says some really positive things. AA teaches us to deal with our own defects of character and treat other people with respect."

Another member, W.B., writes, "After a year in the program, with much support from my two friends and with absolute terror in my heart, I was finally able to talk about being gay with a large group of people at a discussion meeting, and they accepted me as they had come to know me."

With sponsorship, loving fellowship and a Higher Power, the members in this section learned to share and claim their seats in Alcoholics Anonymous.

Pass the Tissues, I've Got Issues
FEBRUARY 1997

In twenty-six years sober and active in AA, I've never once told my story. That's because I'm a gay male alcoholic. In the beginning it was painful to have to try to talk around what really happened. Others could talk about wives, husbands, boyfriends, and girlfriends, but talk about same-sex relations was taboo. In fact, when the first gay group started here in Springfield, announcements about it were greeted with uproarious laughter. Speakers routinely told jokes about queers and fairies and it was considered okay.

Working through the process of self-discovery through identification, for a long time I thought I drank because I didn't feel accepted. I wanted to tell my AA friends how I needed a couple of drinks just to go into a gay bar. Those places scared me to death. I didn't want to be one of "those." Who in his right mind would choose to be different and hated?

For a long time in AA, I believed that acceptance was the answer to all my problems: getting others to accept me. At first I even resisted the little acceptance I got, being so accustomed to rejection or the fear of it. As time went by, I realized that some people were never going to accept me. I know this today and I accept it. After a period of being rebellious and unique, I slowly came to believe that no one could accept me but me.

Gradually I came to a comfortable place where telling my story wasn't all that important. Chapter Five says that "our stories disclose in a general way." I never went to a gay meeting because I didn't join AA to be apart from but a part of.

At the same time I recognized why there was a real need for special groups. If we were really willing to practice love and tolerance, then maybe there wouldn't be. We could all tell our stories in a general way without fear of being socially isolated.

I've been attending a meeting in the five-college area that happens to attract a lot of lesbians and gay males. It's really interesting to be able to look back to a time when we dared not meet in public, to a time now where some of us are so militant and hung up on our differences that the primary work of identification gets lost in all the issues. As the kids in San Francisco like to say, "Pass the tissues. I have issues."

Lately I hear heterosexual males relate that they feel intimidated by the in-your-face feminism that gets displayed at some meetings. I know that gay alcoholics are still hated by many of their straight brothers and sisters. I hear the queer jokes after and before the meeting now. How polite we have become! But our code of love and tolerance is more than just a nice idea. It is a life-extending principle. Bill W. says we want always to be inclusive, never exclusive. And this breaking of the code has ramifications that go far beyond losing one member of AA to hatred and intolerance.

I had the privilege of attending our 60th Anniversary International Convention in San Diego. By accident I walked in on a gay meeting. There had to have been five hundred people there. At first, as I listened to the stories of intolerance, I was sympathetic and grateful that there is finally a place for us where we can belong. But as the meeting progressed I got this feeling of solidarity, esprit de corps, and pride in being different. It concerned me that instead of hearing about recovery from alcoholism, I was hearing what sounded like a call to arms. The meeting ended with the announcement that all the gays were going to sit in the same section of the Jack Murphy stadium for the big sendoff meeting Sunday.

At my meeting today, the subject was sponsorship. As it happened, one woman shared how she picked a gay woman as a sponsor because she felt that someone like herself would "understand." She related how that sponsor just told her what she wanted to hear. The relationship turned personal and then ended. She had to get another sponsor.

In my own experience, I recently acquired a sponsee who happens to be gay. We have a lot in common. We laugh at many of the same things. But he's not really using me as a sponsor. I've had the same problem with heterosexuals. I don't want to hear endlessly about their girlfriends either.

I don't think I need to tell my story in detail, unless there is a compelling reason to do so. People who reveal very personal and sexual aspects of their story from the podium don't realize how distracting these revelations can be. If we continue to talk about incest survival, rape, and problems of sexual identity, what message are we carrying?

I'm not for one minute insensitive to the problems of being different and hated. Anytime I hear people around me telling queer jokes I let them know who they are talking to. I once wrote a letter to a prominent judge who told queer jokes while one of his closest friends, himself a homosexual, died a little with every laugh from the crowd. I told the judge what he had done but not to whom. I wanted him to think about it the next time he felt like getting easy laughs at the expense of others.

So let's remember that the new person needs to make a solid, sober connection through identification with Step One. That message serves our primary purpose and supports our legacies of Recovery, Unity, and Service. Placing personal problems ahead of primary principles can only cause division within our ranks and threaten our future as a movement.

Jim N.
West Springfield, Massachusetts

Whom Do You Hate?
JANUARY 2002 *(From Dear Grapevine)*

Last Labor Day weekend, my partner and I went to an AA round-up. When my sponsor drove up in a truck bearing a rainbow license plate, some people at the round-up made nasty remarks. Later, a fellow alcoholic said, "Dyke," as I walked by. My sponsor left because the vibes were so bad. My partner and I would have left, too, except that we were in an RV, and there were no other campsites to be found that weekend. So we stayed, but we did not feel safe.

I don't think many straight people appreciate how frightening it is to be called names in broad daylight in a public place. The upshot is that I went to an AA function and ended up frightened for my safety and the safety of my family. This happened because someone violated the spirit of AA. We were not being out, or in-your-face. We were trying to stay sober, like every other straight, gay, young, old alcoholic there. So, AA members, the next time you are tempted to say something unkind, try to remember that the person you say it to could be a newcomer, a sponsor, or the voice on the AA hotline who was there when you needed it. Our personal recovery depends upon AA unity, and bigotry and hate erode that unity.

Ren W.
Phoenix, Arizona

A Plea for Love and Tolerance
APRIL 1999 *(From Dear Grapevine)*

I magine going to your home group and being avoided by people with ten or more years of sobriety because they heard you volunteer your time with people with AIDS. Just for a moment, think about what it might be like for a gay man just getting sober to hear someone with "good sobriety" put down gays, blacks, and women. I've been there. I've heard the disparaging remarks about gays and lesbians—in a straight meeting where "love and tolerance is our code." The only reason I stuck around was because I was a hopeless drunk and I had nowhere else to go.

Several years later, I still have a lot of trouble with acceptance. I can't quite accept hearing people with so-called good sobriety tout the Big Book and then put down gays and other minorities in the same sentence. Thank God, there are gay meetings on Long Island, where I can go a couple of times a week and know I'm not going to hear some form of hatred directed at me or others.

The gay meetings I go to are open to anyone. If you show up, you won't hear derogatory remarks being made. And please don't assume that we dilute the message by having a "specialty" meeting. Our primary purpose is to stay sober and help other alcoholics to achieve sobriety.

Jim S.
Hauppauge, New York

I Want to Belong
OCTOBER 1977

I am sitting at my group's Thursday-night speaker meeting with about 200 other sober AAs, laughing and forgetting myself. I hear the speaker remind me what it was like, what happened, and how it is now. In the nearly seven years since I had my last drink, I have learned how to belong and how to feel a part of something bigger than I am, something decent and worthwhile.

All of a sudden, in the middle of a string of bright, humorous asides, the speaker gets an easy laugh telling about some "fag" or "queer" from his past. It hits me like cold water. I am always a little shocked to hear my people laughing, because I am one of those "queers" they're laughing at.

Once again, I feel put out of the meeting. I again remember what I had forgotten: that I do not belong as much as I would like to think. I get over it, of course. I tell myself that, after all, habits are hard to break. And then, not everybody laughed. Still, I am afraid to look to see who did. It might be somebody I love with the love that AA taught me.

When they started a gay AA group in our area, the announcement drew laughter, usually started by one person, and one night the meeting was turned almost into a circus with the hilarity that ensued. Interestingly enough, that night three new people had stood up to say that this was their first meeting. What an impression they got of AA!

Thank God, the first speaker took five preliminary minutes to say something about it before he told his story. "I suppose we all had a good laugh at that announcement," he began, "but I for one don't think it's a bit funny. I wonder what would have happened to me if people had laughed at me at my first meeting."

I was grateful to him that night for his courage and told him so. So did several others. Who better than sober AAs should understand the pain of exclusion? When are we going to grow up in AA?

I did not join that gay group, partly from fear of being "found out," but also because I did not come here to stay apart. I want to belong to all of AA and the whole human race. This is the promise of sobriety as I understand it. It is what I continue to struggle for, and to be hurt for. I believe in this promise.

Sometimes, when they start with the queer jokes, I want to jump up and yell out, "I am one of those queers you all think are so funny. Does anybody here know me? Does anybody care that that word goes through me like a knife?" But I don't. True, my laughter is interrupted a little. But after the meeting, I join my fellows in the silent conspiracy against myself and try to get back the feeling that I belong.

J. N.
Massachusetts

Special Groups
FEBRUARY 1981 *(Excerpt from Dear Grapevine)*

We AAs are all united by our alcoholism, but there is still a lot of room for diversity in our Fellowship. Some of that diversity is expressed in special groups—men, women, young people, etc. This has gone on since AA's early days, presumably with the blessing of the founders (for example, see the story of Jim S. on page 483 of the third edition of the Big Book).

My home group is one of about twenty gay groups in Seattle. Being gay and male was an important part of my life as a practicing drunk, and dealing with life as a gay man is an important part of my recovery in AA. However, there is no such thing as "gay AA." There is only AA, and some meetings consist mostly of gay recovering alcoholics.

J. K.
Seattle, Washington

The Support We All Need
JANUARY 1980 *(Excerpt)*

The speaker drawled, "And honey, you just keep your hanths off me. You're definitely *not* my type." He flicked a limp wrist at his audience and mimicked the popular stereotype of the gay male. His audience laughed. A stand-up comic on a 1960s variety show? No, a speaker at a large open meeting of Alcoholics Anonymous. And five gay recovering alcoholics who were there looked at one another and didn't laugh.

"In this organization, we don't keep anybody out. Why, we've got ex-cons, maybe murderers, thieves, hookers, junkies. We've even got some queers." A recruiter for the local chapter of the Down-and-Outers? No, a recovering alcoholic leading a meeting on the Third Tradition. One gay recovering alcoholic never returned to that meeting, and two others resolved even more firmly to keep their sexual preference the guilty secret it had always been.

Are these isolated instances of thoughtless comments at meetings? Not in my own experience. I am a gay recovering alcoholic who has been sober for three and one-half years, and during that time, at what must by now be something over a thousand meetings that I have attended, I have heard more "faggot" jokes (as well as other pointless put-downs of various minorities) than I hear in my day-to-day work environment. How do I handle it? Sometimes, not very well. I get angry and I take other peoples' inventories. But most of the time, I repeat to myself the Twelfth Tradition, and finally get my head straightened out and my anger turned into something that is often, quite frankly, grudging acceptance.

But what about the gay alcoholic who is just coming into the program? What about the gay man or woman who has been told that he or she will find compassion, acceptance, help, support, and love from a group of people who have something that he or she wants? My experience in working with other gay recovering alcoholics, both in and out of my own gay AA group, is that their reaction is not good; that they are often turned off by the whole program of AA because of a few comments; that they don't "keep coming back"; that AA members seem to them just like everyone else in the world—full of prejudices and unwilling to accept individual differences, whatever they may be.

I sobered up in a "straight" group in a moderately large town. In looking back over the first terrifying weeks of sobriety, in thinking about the meetings I attended, in reviewing the conversations I had with several people who became my close friends, in recalling the kinds of comments that I often heard made about gay men and women, I can honestly say that if I hadn't had two people who accepted me from the start as gay, I might not have sobered up at all. One of the men is himself gay, and the two of us talked about our problems and went to meetings together, never able to share completely with the other members of the group. The other man, my sponsor, is straight, and I might have been the first gay man with whom he had ever talked seriously. But he knew the program and carried it into all of his affairs. He kept saying, "Hang on. 'Principles before personalities.' Someday, you'll be able to talk about your sexual preference."

My continuing sobriety was absolutely dependent, in the long run, on complete honesty, and that honesty obviously involved my sexuality and my lifestyle. After a year in the program, with much support from my two friends and with absolute terror in my heart, I was finally able to talk about being gay with a large group of people at a discussion meeting, and they accepted me as they had come to know me. The "faggot" jokes stopped at our meetings, because everyone had finally met an authentic "faggot" and discovered that he was just like any other recovering alcoholic—hurting, confused, in desperate need of their help and acceptance, and willing to pay with honesty any price that was necessary.

Three weeks ago at a conference, I heard someone say, "The trouble with queers is that they think they are different and need special treatment." The only special treatment that most of us ask is the special treatment that the Big Book suggests for all recovering alcoholics. I don't expect anyone to "understand" my problems, because I don't understand many of them myself. All I ask is that they accept me for me, and that they give me the support we all need in getting sober.

W. B.
Norman, Oklahoma

One Primary Purpose
AUGUST 1997 *(Excerpt from Dear Grapevine)*

As a recovering alcoholic who happens to be a gay male, I can't stress enough the importance of gay special interest meetings, in addition to non-special interest meetings. An important part of my recovery has been the ability to tell my story, unabridged. Due to my own character defects and my perception that there are prejudices in the world, I find this difficult to do at non-special interest groups.

Tradition Five says, "Each group has but one primary purpose—to carry its message to the alcoholic who still suffers." I would like to say that this is true at gay as well as non-special interest meetings that I attend.

Jim S.
Maryland

Just How Welcome Are You?
JUNE 1996

Are gay men welcome to attend meetings for men only? Recently, after a distressing day spent battling the desire to drink again, I braved the cold and gratefully parked myself at one of our tables with a cup of hot coffee and awaited the start of a much-needed meeting. I'd recently moved to this city, and I selected this meeting because of its proximity to my new home. The schedule indicated a meeting for men only. No problem, I thought. I'm a man.

In the five minutes before the Serenity Prayer, however, two vulgar and insulting jokes about "faggots" were told, and most of the men reacted with boisterous laughter. I felt shock and panic. Was I safe in that room? Would I be physically harmed if I objected? I decided to remain silent and seated, since I desperately needed a meeting and was afraid of what I would do if I left with a bitter resentment. The men telling the jokes were tactless, to be certain, but I believed that once the meeting began, the spirit of Alcoholics Anonymous would bring us all together compassionately in our quest for sobriety and serenity. Naturally they practiced our principles in all their affairs. Surely they carried out the First Tradition and practiced the Twelve Steps collectively.

I couldn't have been more mistaken. During the discussion, one man made a detestable, unrepeatable comment about AIDS and gay men, as if no heterosexual had ever died in the epidemic. Again, I made excuses to myself in order to stay at the meeting: I'm HIV-negative; he isn't talking about me. These men have no idea I'm gay or even who I am; these comments aren't directed at me personally.

As if in response to my absurd rationalization, toward the end of the meeting, another man stated undisguisedly that he hated "all those damned gays." At that point I ran out of excuses for the group. Thankfully, the meeting was nearly finished.

I stopped at a service station after I left to call my new sponsor, a straight man free of hatred and bigotry. He invited me over to his place for a hug and a chat with him and his wife, both of whom are long-time AA members. They always have time to share with those of us in need of love or advice. Patiently they waited out my angry raving and guided me back to serenity and sober reasoning. My sponsor suggested that I cool off for a week and pray for serenity. Now, with his blessing and with the guidance of my Higher Power, I would like to make a suggestion for the mens' meetings in our city and elsewhere: take a group inventory.

Are you carrying the message to *all* alcoholic men? Are you practicing the principles of AA in your meeting? Do you intentionally use vicious, excluding language before, during, or after the meeting? Are you remembering that we are all just one drink away from what could be a fatal slip? Might your gay-hating comments be driving away newcomers?

In many cities, groups for gay men do exist. When a straight man unknowingly walks into an AA meeting primarily for gay men, I would hope the group conscience would encourage him to stay, as long as he respects us and our anonymity. Will your heterosexual mens' group be able to extend the same courtesy to gay men in desperate need of a meeting?

Hank S.
Lafayette, Indiana

A Rare Value
OCTOBER 2000 *(From Your Move)*

I was very interested in the articles in the May issue regarding the Third Tradition. I am one of a handful of openly gay men in the northern area of Minnesota. I have over eighteen years of sobriety, got sober in a major urban area, and have been to AA meetings all over the U.S. and Canada. I did most of my drinking and drug use in one of America's largest gay ghettos. I got sober at a gay AA club. I have also been going to predominantly straight AA meetings since my first week in the program.

One good thing the gay AA group did was have a lot of discussion about the Third Tradition. Very early in the program I was told that people had the right to go to any AA meeting they wanted, and what the other attendees at the group felt was their issue, not mine. I didn't then, and don't now, feel the need to have majority approval of my lifestyle to feel good about myself. When you are a member of a minority, not everyone is going to like you.

There is a fair degree of prejudice up here. But there is a fair degree of prejudice about a lot of things everywhere. Welcome to the species.

Alcoholics Anonymous is probably the only organization in this community that is open to anyone who wishes to attend. Tolerance is a very rare value in our society. AA's policy of tolerance says some really positive things. AA teaches us to deal with our own defects of character and treat other people with respect.

Stephen S.
Duluth, Minnesota

Is Our Message for Everyone?
OCTOBER 1991 *(Excerpt)*

Sobriety has saved my life, and in Alcoholics Anonymous I am learning a great many things. More than ever I desire the spiritual life of awakening and giving and receiving that the Twelve Steps offer. In many ways my story is exactly like that of any other person who has experienced the miracle of life through the program. I love AA.

But I am a lesbian. And while I sat and listened to this woman tell a story not so different from mine, I thought again about the times well-meaning people in AA have encouraged me not to talk about my intimate relationships at meetings, that being gay was an "outside" issue.

It scares me to think my story of recovery matters less to AA because I'm not straight and not lying about it to protect anyone. But what scares me more are the drunk, alienated, suffering lesbian and gay alcoholics out there in the world, who don't *see* recovery for themselves in AA because they don't hear about sobriety from lesbian and gay people behind the podium. They sense that they will always be outsiders, even in AA.

It's been estimated that one in three gay people is alcoholic, and that one person out of ten is gay. That's a staggering suggestion. Is AA now willing—or will we ever be willing—to help all these people recover and to be helped *by* them? Is our message of hope really for everyone?

I am sober today and in service for my group because AA gave me life and God and hope, and because I want the hand of AA always to be extended for the next suffering drunk. In that way, I'm not different. I want AA for myself and for others.

But does AA really want me?

Karen L.
Durham, North Carolina

Response to "Is Our Message for Everyone?"
FEBRUARY 1992 *(From Dear Grapevine)*

I feel compelled to write after reading Karen L.'s article, "Is Our Message for Everyone?" in the October Grapevine. Speaking for myself as the miniscule part of AA that I represent, yes, Karen, AA really does want you. More than that, we need you.

Is AA really going to start rejecting people on the basis of their sexual orientation? What's next, no blacks, no Jews, no dirty or active alcoholics who smell bad?

One of the most powerful spiritual experiences I have had the privilege to be a part of took place at a retreat for male AAs about a year ago. I was asked to lead the retreat's Saturday night meeting, and one of the two speakers was a young man named Bill whom I had met on a previous retreat.

As all those who have attended them know, retreats can be wonderful, revitalizing experiences. However, since this was an all-male gathering, there was a certain amount of that macho posturing and locker-room bravado that occurs whenever you get a large group of men—or boys—together.

At the meeting, Bill stood up in front of this group of some 100 men and shared his experience, strength, and hope with us. His story included his wrenching and painful struggle to come to grips with his own sexual identity and how alcohol and drug use were intricately tied up in them. I got the impression that this was the first time he had ever publicly spoken about his homosexuality in front of a group of straight alcoholics.

I cannot describe how moved I was by this man's courage and strength. I was able to identify with so much of Bill's story; the fact that he was a homosexual and I was not was irrelevant. Bill is facing physical and emotional pain in his life that I just don't know if I could handle. And he is doing it with a dignity that I doubt many people of any sexual persuasion could duplicate. He says the source of much of his strength is the rooms of AA. Tell me, should we try to take that away from him? Is that what Bill W. and Dr. Bob would want us to do?

So, yes, Karen, AA really does want you, at least the way I see it. And like I said, more than that, we need you.

M. M.
Carmel, New York

CHAPTER 7

LIFE ON LIFE'S TERMS

*Using the Twelve Steps and the Fellowship to deal with
adversity, illness and loss*

How do you handle adversity—a financial crisis, serious illness, or the death of a loved one—when drinking is no longer an option? When his actively alcoholic brother dies in his first year of sobriety, Nick K.'s sponsor reminds him that he is the only sober person in his family. He is the one who ends up arranging the funeral, but he goes to meetings every day. "At each meeting, I cried. At each meeting, people held my hand," Nick writes. "I didn't realize the power of AA."

"I began to see a part of the Fellowship I never knew existed," writes Kyle R. about the death of his partner to an AIDS-related illness. "I was physically and emotionally taken care of ... I know now that I can survive tragedy without drinking."

In this chapter, AAs dealing with adversity show how reaching out a hand to other members, or simply accepting the support offered to them, means they don't have to bear the pain alone. And they get through it, sober.

A Death in the Family
FEBRUARY 2004

What is that saying—when God closes a door, he opens a window? I have found this to be true in my life since getting sober. I have been sober since May 1996. With the help of a sponsor who told me what to do, and by attending many meetings, being of service, helping others, praying, listening to other sober people and working the Steps, I am living a life beyond my wildest dreams. If you had asked me during my first year of sobriety, I would not have been so positive about my AA experience.

I come from a family of alcoholics and people addicted to "more." I was raised in Philadelphia with my two older brothers, and each of us developed our own addiction. Fortunately, mine didn't bloom until I was in college. My middle brother was not so lucky. He died three times from his addiction before he finally died in May 1997.

I was at a graduation for a friend from the program. Tiffany was my "sober buddy." We were both young, gay, and trying to start a new way of life while finishing up college. She had won a special award and I was sitting at her "family" table, because no one from her family had shown up. I had a strange feeling of urgency to get home to my parents' house, because I knew something was going on. I waited until after her award was presented and eventually bowed out, heading home on a hunch.

When I got home, I found both of my parents crying hysterically in the living room. My mother couldn't look at me. My father could only say "It happened. Your brother is dead." I remember not feeling surprised or overwhelmed by grief at that time. I sat with them and tried to comfort them as best I could. My other brother got the news and went to the bar. I went up to my bedroom and called my sponsor.

I was fortunate to have a wonderful sponsor who went to all

lengths to help me get sober. My sponsor was not home. I left him a message saying I needed to talk to him right away. When he called me back, I told him that Chris was dead. When I heard his voice, I finally felt safe enough to let down my guard and I cried and cried. My sponsor told me to ask my family what they needed me to do to help them prepare for the funeral, and he reminded me that I was the only sober person in my family. I knew what this meant.

The first horrible task was to tell my brother's children that their father was dead. My six-year old nephew listened to me explain how his father was an angel, and finally interrupted me. "So he's dead," my nephew said. I told him yes. All he wanted was to go home and be with his mother.

Each night of that week, someone else in AA gave me a different commitment. One night, I had to open the church. Another night, I had to drive a newcomer to the meeting. Another night, I had to speak. Another night, make coffee. And so I went through the motions of the days, burying my brother, having a mass and a wake, and each night going to a meeting. At each meeting, I cried. At each meeting, people held my hand.

I didn't realize the power of AA or sobriety at that point. I didn't know that AA was a winning lottery ticket. The payback for me has been a range of emotions, choices, friends, faith, family, responsibility, and self-respect. Time goes by, and each May I remember my brother and it is bittersweet at my anniversary time. But all the things that have happened in my life have been a gift.

Now, I live with a wonderful partner in Maryland. I am active in AA, have a new and equally wonderful sponsor, reach out my hand to others, work the Steps, and pray. Most importantly though, I never forget. I don't forget the faces of the people who helped me through that horrible week. I don't forget to offer that support when someone else needs it. I don't know their names anymore, but our exchange was beyond words.

I know that this opportunity to live a life riding a winning lottery ticket is not cashed in by each person who tries AA. I don't know why I got sober and my brother did not. I don't know why AA works. I just know that I am sober and grateful today, and I hope I die sober. But there is little I can do to control the future, so when I lay my head down and pray tonight I will again thank God for the fortune I have received. And when I die, I can't wait to tell Chris about how wonderful life can be.

Nick K.
Joppa, Maryland

Staying Sober—No Matter What
JULY 1992

R oy and I were both in jail for drunk and disorderly charges back in 1987 when we got together. I got out before he did, swearing I would stop drinking so I wouldn't lose him. I promised to change. I was back in jail that night. Roy said either I straightened out or he would walk, and that ultimatum began our journey in AA.

In July of 1987 I came here to Kingston, and by the grace of God got sober. Roy came up the following December, too. It was a relationship no one thought would work. Our counselors thought we should end the relationship, but I knew in my heart that if Roy threatened my sobriety, I would give him up. I was prepared to let go, but I didn't have to.

We enjoyed four years together, immersed in AA and getting on with our lives. Even when Roy was diagnosed HIV positive in 1988, we kept our faith in God and in the Fellowship and kept on with our programs. We enjoyed life together, sober and clean. We both went to college and did well.

In November 1990 Roy began to get sick. He lost weight and developed skin discolorations. I think he was often very sick, though he never really shared with me what was happening. But I knew the disease was claiming him though sometimes my denial would not allow me to face it. We worked very hard at maintaining our separate programs and Roy kept going to meetings and being involved.

On December 31, 1991 Roy celebrated three years sober. He could barely walk to the podium, but he did. I had the clear thought that I'd never see him celebrate another anniversary. One week later he was gone.

Then the real program of AA came through to me as I began to see a part of the Fellowship I never knew existed. I was physically and emotionally taken care of. My sponsor said that you give and give and give, and sometimes you just need to sit back and take. Well, I took. From that first night, I was not alone. My sponsor and three close friends drove me to the hospital at 1 A.M. to say good-bye to Roy. Afterward we sat and drank coffee. I was in shock. I felt as if my soul was wrenched from me. What would I do without Roy? Everything I saw reminded me of him and brought fresh tears and agony. How could I possibly stay sober through such pain and loss?

Finally, it was meeting time. I'm the coffee-maker for the 7 A.M. meeting and after making the coffee, I quietly pulled people aside and told them that Roy had gone. Before the meeting, I asked a friend if I should bring up a topic, and she said, "Are you kidding?" And I knew I had to share. I raised my hand. I said that Roy had passed away that morning, and I didn't know what to do. "How can I face going home to an empty apartment?" I cried.

By the end of that hour, even those who didn't know Roy directly were visibly moved. I had never felt such love and encouragement as I felt that morning. I knew I wasn't alone. For the next three days, my apartment was filled with people, some who took off from work just to spend a day with me. My friends went shopping and made dinner, forcing me to eat. They walked my dog, cleaned my house, gave me money, and helped make the funeral arrangements.

I spent the first day on the phone, calling everybody I knew. No sooner would I hang up than someone would call, saying they had just heard about Roy, and did I need anything? Was I all right? I don't know—I was in shock, and being on the telephone was therapy for me. It gave me something to do, and it helped galvanize the truth in my soul—Roy was gone, and here were these people, soulmates in fellowship, as testimony to his absence.

The sorrow was palpable at meetings that week as we shared our loss. We needed to talk about the pain. It was time for crying and weeping silently, for sadness and relief that he didn't have to suffer the excruciating loss of health and dignity that so many do.

For me, it was a time of growth, of an emergence into the world of reality where the pink cloud dissipates, and the awful truth sets in: Bad things do happen to good people, and we don't understand why, and maybe there aren't any answers, and the best we can do is to go on and find our niche in the scheme of things. Maybe, I thought, there is an answer, but it's not for me to know.

We had a ceremony for Roy. Close to 200 AA friends came to support me and express love for Roy. We stood in our darkest hour to see Roy in his brightest moment. I read a letter from Roy's mother. She expressed gratitude to our friends for the love we gave Roy, and she was proud of him for his sobriety. Then I was lost for words. We closed the meeting with a moment of silence for Roy, followed by the Serenity Prayer. The emotion was overwhelming, and I became aware of a change within me. I know now that I can survive tragedy without drinking.

I remember one member spoke of his continuing relationship to God as a dog listening to Beethoven. The dog hears something, but has no comprehension of what it is or what it means. That's how I think of God as well. I know God is there and sometimes is so close I can hear or feel him, but I'll never be able to comprehend it.

I don't know the music, but there is sound—sometimes rushing and furious, sometimes gentle and caressing. But always there's the sound of a master pianist at play, conducting some mad orchestra of life. I don't know what or why or how, but I know I'm here. And the best I can do is to find God's will for me.

I don't know why Roy had to go. What God does or doesn't do is none of my business. That's why I'm mortal. I have no bitterness, no anger. Ten months later, I can actually see it as a tragic blessing. Roy had AA friends with him at the hospital, and they told me he was ready to go. That brought me peace. I knew that before Roy closed his eyes he saw the grace of God and was secure in where he was and where he was going. He died sober.

Yes, it still hurts, and I still cry. But I'm sober, and by God's grace, I will celebrate five years in July. And as painful as the memories are, I am grateful to remember. I spent five years in a perpetual blackout; now I can remember.

Kyle R.
Kingston, New York

Here I Am
FEBRUARY 1976

I am a human being, alcoholic, homosexual, pill-head, and laryngectomee. Man, what a title! Better than the ones I used to label myself with. I am sharing with you to let all know this program works as long as I believe in my Higher Power, whom I call Herhim. (Don't know whether H.P. is a he, she, it, or what!)

It took me a long time to realize I was not so damn unique. Before that, I could not stay sober, not because of AA, but because of me. My sponsor suggested that I hold my hand out with love and that I surrender. I did both and found out that I was able to admit, accept, and surrender and to love this program and the people in it. Without the love of "straight" people in AA and a few other "gays" in the program, I would not be sober today. My Herhim gave me the ability to love and share.

After thirteen years of sobriety, I found I had throat cancer, so I had to have a laryngectomy, and life since then has not been easy. I may soon be able to learn how to talk again. People in AA shared their strength and love and sent cards, both in the hospital and after I got home. There have been times when I wanted to give up, but each time I called someone. A Sacramento AA and his wife gave me great support, as he is a living example of staying sober and learning how to talk. He also had a laryngectomy. I ate my first regular meal at an anniversary of his group here in Sacramento. The courage I gained in seeing Ed eat and talk gave me the strength to try. Through the help of the AA program, my Herhim, and people in AA, I did not have to drink, pop a pill, cut a wrist, or slam a hand through a door with frustration. I hope to make my fourteenth anniversary two months from now.

I will hold my head up with respect and love for myself. I was a hard-nosed butch who had, not merely a chip, but a whole tree of hate on her shoulder. Thanks to Herhim, I have mellowed. Here I am, you straights. Let me love and understand you, so I can love and understand me, so we can love and understand each other.

At some of the meetings, the so-called straights, who I was sure hated me, now ask me to write down on a piece of paper what I can share, and they read it aloud for me and then say, "This is for Kel." One group (women only) agreed not to smoke one evening, so I could attend. (You see, smoke will bother me very much until I heal completely.) Other AAs pick me up and take me to meetings. Some came to the house and held a meeting for me after I got out of the hospital—and hey, you AAs—they were not a gay group.

Get the message, get into the program, and hold your hand out and love, one drunk to another. God bless all of you.

K. L.
Sacramento, California

The Gift that Never Dies
AUGUST 2006

Meeting Bernie didn't seem like an encounter that would so completely change my life. He was a bouncer in a bar, hired to get rid of exactly the sort I was: a twenty-seven-year-old washout of a drunk. At first glance, we seemed very different. Most noticeably, he was straight and I was gay. However, he spotted a similarity far more fundamental. We were both alcoholics. To Bernie, the only important difference was his spiritual recovery facing my own insane denial.

I found out later that he immediately pegged me as an overripe Twelfth-Step call. Slowly, annoyingly, and with much humor, Bernie extended the hand of AA to me exactly the way it is laid out in the Big Book. He told me his story, which went on and on. When I started to drift, he bought me another drink. That was all I needed to feign a little more interest.

Over some weeks, I developed a real interest in this poor guy's endless drunkalog. In my confusion, I asked some fateful questions: "You don't drink, do you?" "How long has it been?" Short answers were quickly followed by elaborate stories of his drinking and equally elaborate pipe-lighting pauses. In one of those long pauses, I started wondering about myself. As a rule, I didn't go in for self-reflection, and certainly didn't like thinking about my drinking. As he launched into an epic about how he and a drinking buddy ruined a business, I thought that, like him, I had never had just one.

As a toddler, I first tasted alcohol from my father's beer can. My dad had been seriously wounded in World War II and collected a psychiatric disability check until he died. I thought the world of him and drank from his ever-present can of beer on those rare occasions when my mother's only option was to leave her children in his care. They fought constantly. My mom was always very sad while trying to be cheerful; my dad held the world in contempt while he drank.

Even before I became a teenager, I viewed drinking as something important that I liked to do. I needed it and figured I had a right to it, like playing sports and singing, or reading the news and history books. I got into trouble pretty regularly because my drinking and drugging were worrisome to other people. They didn't understand that, although I was young, I could handle it. By my twentieth year, a number of my gang had died, proving me right. It wasn't me who had died of a suicide, car crash, or overdose. I was fine. I left Pittsburgh behind and moved to New York to live as an adult. Finally, I was free to be gay, free to drink as I pleased.

My lover and I got an apartment on the Upper West Side of Manhattan. I had known David since high school, and we seemed to complement each other. He was a piano player and I was a singer. He was a vegetarian and I loved steaks. He cultivated friendships; I didn't. He never drank. We both wanted to create a family and even adopted a homeless teenager. We fought constantly.

When I was twenty-three, my mother died. The character of my drinking changed. Slowly at first, but more and more joylessly, I became a desperation drinker. I no longer needed "a few" or even just to get drunk. I needed oblivion. I wanted to erase myself. My drinking had long been important; now it held a position in my life that overshadowed all else. At home, on a job, or in pursuit of my career, I just went through the motions and I knew it. A part of me said I should care about not caring, but I was powerless.

I landed a job in a Broadway show and, while having a drink in my fifth-floor dressing room, the emptiness of it all nearly made me jump out the window on opening night. A year earlier, a reviewer had written of my singing that, although it had a pleasant sound, "Dan is, however, strangely dead behind the eyes." I agreed but couldn't imagine what to do about it. I didn't even know what the problem was.

Maybe I was the problem. Because Bernie left me out while telling his story, it fell to me to develop the shocking concept that maybe I, too, was an alcoholic. Even after my questioning led Bernie to nonchalantly acknowledge that it was AA that finally brought his drinking story to a conclusion, he still only spoke of himself.

He said that he couldn't tell me if I was an alcoholic. I'd have to answer that myself. An AA meeting didn't sound like fun, but as a fact-finding mission it rose to tolerable. I just hoped that David didn't find out. He had just started going to Al-Anon, and I didn't want him to think that he was right.

I began going to meetings but didn't fully surrender for another four and a half years of misery. I got ninety days several times and even hit the six-month mark once. Each time I drank again, it was a disaster.

I kept going back to AA to get myself together. Inevitably, after finding another job or patching things up with David, I'd think I didn't need meetings or a sponsor. What I really needed was a drink. By the spring of 1985, I was in a constant grayout. I had liver damage from drinking with hepatitis. I didn't have a job and was obviously unemployable. I had no friends left and acquaintances made a point of avoiding me. I had signed away rights to my apartment in an indignant blackout rage, and David had changed the locks. I was, for all practical purposes, homeless. I slept many nights in Central Park.

I stumbled into a few meetings because I didn't know what else to do. I had gotten used to the routine of going to meetings to help me quit drinking for a while. That no longer worked. I became so hopeless that I actually prayed for the guts to kill myself.

Bernie found me in an empty apartment I had broken into. He knew I needed to detox for a few days. He also knew that if I got some food down I'd pass out for a long rest.

I woke up, shaking badly and very thirsty. Bernie was still there. I was amazed and horrified. He said he was staying. At one point, with all the indignation I could muster, I told him he was doing this all wrong. "I'm supposed to want to get sober and I don't! So just leave!" (I had heard something in those meetings.) Ten minutes later, sobbing, I begged him not to look at me. I never want anyone to see me like that again. After another day or two of crying and shaking, we went to a meeting, then on to his apartment where I stayed in his gym (a tiny room strewn with barbells and a wrestling mat to sleep on). I woke up one morning and overheard him telling his sponsor on the phone, "Yeah, I got Dan here, sleeping with the other dumbbells."

I was now willing to go to any lengths to stay sober. "Don't drink and go to meetings" became my mantra. I went to tons of meetings and never missed the Midnight Meeting on 46th Street. I loved that meeting not only for its extreme eccentricities, but because it was there, among the most desperate alcoholics, that I understood that "not drinking" was not a substitute for drinking.

I kept resisting Bernie's suggestion that we do what he called an active Third Step. He wanted me to pray. Specifically, he wanted me to say the Third Step Prayer from the Big Book with him. I told him I couldn't. The idea of addressing God in such a personal way and in the presence of another person made me unbearably conscious of the overwhelming shame of my life. I hated myself for being all that I really was, and especially for being gay. Bernie said okay. He would say his prayers and go to bed.

While he prayed, I still had the Big Book open to the prayer that begins: "God I offer myself to thee ..." I said the full prayer in earnest. I immediately felt an interior shift. It hurt to offer the vague lump of shame and fear that I was to God. What was transforming about this prayer was to hear for the first time my true inner voice longing for God to take me and build with me—as well as the added blessing of realizing that I believed he would. I was sober and sincerely asking to be relieved of the unbearable burden of self. Having the Third Step in my life made all the difference. I gained access to an inner life that put me firmly on the path to a spiritually-based life and recovery. I no longer needed to substitute anything for drinking. I was recovering myself and gaining access to the genuine experience of my own life. Thank God.

It was on a Wednesday afternoon in my third year of sobriety that my doctor called with the news that, as suspected, I was HIV positive. He added that my immune system was already severely compromised. Although this news was not entirely unexpected, I was stunned. I hung up the phone and it rang immediately. I had forgotten that a good AA pal waited on the other line for the news. We discussed it for a while and Bob suggested we go to that evening's Lambda meeting. From the very first minute of my personal struggle with AIDS, my Higher Power was there in the form of AA.

I went to the meeting that night and told my friends the news. It was 1987. We were terrified and already reeling from the crisis we found ourselves in.

Lambda was a special interest meeting of Alcoholics Anonymous for gay men and lesbians—but where all with a desire to stop drinking were welcome. More than half of the men I'd met there over the last thirteen years were dead of AIDS. It was a meeting where I felt safe enough to bring my shame and ugliest self-loathing. It was at this meeting, with these people, that I began to retake possession of basic human dignity.

Of the many who are now gone, the one I think of most often is my dear friend, David S. Our AA kind of friendship, a kind of non-sexual intimacy, taught me how to love myself on ever-deepening levels. By watching him through his horrible illness and death, I learned a way of observing myself without judgment. His death and the deaths of so many others, while my own has hovered near, is the kind of big experience that is a gift with a duty. A duty to report that sober, in God's world, grief and loss must not be denied. The gift of an inner life where God is present, and self-love and acceptance are genuine. And, as Bernie knew so well, the gift never dies when it is passed on and on.

I, myself, seem to go on and on. Continuing to live with AIDS is quite an adventure. Only God knows the last chapter to that story. And, when I'm in a meeting, or anywhere with alcoholics, I go on about a variety of good stuff. I talk on about the AA kind of love founded in esteem and compassion, rather than need or pity. I talk about gathering a bigger, more authentic self by embracing the grief and lamenting the losses of my life. Most of all, I talk about the miracle of my sobriety. I don't drink and I don't even want to. AA, as David S. liked to tell newcomers, "works fine. Just fine."

Dan C.
New York, New York
Note: Dan C. celebrated his last sober anniversary on May 29,
2004, with 19 years of sobriety. He died seven months later.

Sober at 63
APRIL 2010

Give in! Give in! Just drink and die! I actually thought that would be the easiest way out—to drink myself to death. But it didn't happen that way.

My life was in turmoil—I hated myself and felt I had arrived at a dead end. Alcohol became my way out. If I drank enough, I didn't care anymore. Easy solution! So I began to drink daily, stopping at the package store every afternoon on the way home from work—of course, not the same package store each day. I wouldn't want them to know I was a heavy hitter, after all. Too soon, half pints became pints and more, with bottles hidden under the front seat of my car.

In 2003, I retired and had even more time to drink. Savings bonds were cashed and retirement money evaporated quickly into my disease. Frightening blackouts were a nightly occurrence and I began to pray for help. But knowing that I had a problem didn't push me into recovery.

It wasn't until June 2004, when a friend I was visiting confided in me that she was going to AA meetings, that I was able to face my disease squarely. My questions prompted her to ask if I'd like to go with her, and I attended my first AA meeting on June 28, 2004. I was 63 years old.

And so the journey began. My Higher Power had heard my prayers! I was willing to do whatever it took to get sober. Guided by good sponsors, I began to change.

Hoping that my partner and former drinking buddy would also join AA, my sponsor and I encouraged her participation in Al-Anon and in the AA social gatherings, but as I became more involved in AA, she became angrier and continued to drink heavily. Heeding my sponsor's words, "Don't make any major changes in the first year," I stayed the course until it became apparent that my safety was threatened.

Running away from home at age 65 was an eye-opener. Because my finances were tied to joint accounts, there was no money to use as I saw fit. HP provided, but I needed to do some footwork and humble myself by asking others for help. AA friends were there for me. First my brother, also an AA member, opened his home to me. That month with him gave me some alone time to become physically and mentally strong, and AA meetings kept me spiritually fit.

It was then that I was offered the opportunity to care for a dear AA friend who was dying of cancer. My year and eight months as her caregiver were a godsend. I was provided with room and board and a stipend. As I cooked, cleaned and cared for my friend, AA came to me. I was constantly surrounded by AA friends, visits and support.

One day at a time, I've learned to live in the now. And so I continue the journey. The Promises I heard at my first AA meeting have been realized in so many ways and I am truly happy, joyous and free—thanks to AA.

Rita C.
Wimauma, Florida

CHAPTER 8

ENJOYING LIFE MORE THAN EVER BEFORE

The joy of living through working the AA program

There are many ways to experience happiness through sobriety and AA. There's a warm glow that results when using the Steps and Traditions that leads to better relationships with others. There's the laughter of friends traveling or camping together. There's the exuberance, love and joy shared at an AA convention. And there's the new connection with others that results from letting go of old beliefs and behaviors and embracing new ones.

"As I grew in the program," writes one member, "many of my intense personal feelings of guilt, fear, and isolation began to fade. I began to see AA as a truly nonjudgmental program of personal recovery, and a fellowship of equals."

As another member writes, "Today, as a result of attending both gay and other meetings, I am a happier alcoholic. My circle of friends has expanded tremendously."

The stories in this chapter show how LGBT alcoholics are recovering from alcoholism, becoming part of the Alcoholics Anonymous family, and enjoying life more than ever before.

In All Our Affairs
APRIL 2005

Our Friday evening AA meeting started innocently enough. The format called for a member to read a brief selection out of the Big Book. I had volunteered, and read from the chapter "Into Action," beginning with the sentence, "Love and tolerance of others is our code. And we have ceased fighting anything or anyone—even alcohol." Following the reading, the chairperson asked if anyone had a topic to suggest. When no one spoke up, he suggested "love and tolerance."

This being election time in the U.S., several members of our group (a gay group) had been heatedly talking politics before the meeting, which included some fairly emotional bashing of the political opposition. So, when the meeting started, the theme of "love and tolerance" was quickly appropriated and applied to the world of partisan politics. The first few people to share tried to walk that fine line we all must walk when it comes to talking about potentially explosive topics. But the fourth person who shared said that he would pass along voter registration forms and requests for absentee ballots while the meeting continued.

It's easy to imagine how quickly things got out of hand as, one by one, almost every AA Tradition was at least bent, if not broken. Near the end of the meeting, one of the long-time members spoke passionately about how inappropriate the whole topic had been, and how such a meeting could easily drive away any newcomer who might think that the only requirement for membership was to be a registered member of a specific political party. The member who read the Promises at the end of the meeting nearly cried. And when the meeting ended, many of the members congregated outside on the sidewalk, talking about how they now really needed an AA meeting.

I found that I couldn't sleep well that night: the meeting haunted me. I reexamined what I had shared, looking for what I might have done to prevent the meltdown that occurred. And actually, what had happened? Of course, it goes without saying that discussing our individual view of partisan politics in an AA meeting is inappropriate. But discussing how we deal with the strongly held opinions and beliefs engendered by partisan politics—how it affects our emotional sobriety and how we work our program when we're "worked up"—is not. It's just like any other life issue that we face sober. I also think that it's just as amenable to discussion as any other topic. In a meeting, we're looking for ways to grow spiritually as well as looking for ways to apply the principles of the program in our lives so that we may stay sober.

It seems to me that there are some areas of our lives as sober people—most notably politics, religion, and sex—that are difficult to deal with. Indeed, discussions of such topics can lead the best of people to permanent rifts with family, friends, or colleagues. Over my twenty-three years in AA, I can't recall a single meeting where the topic of how we integrate the principles of our recovery program into our lives as political citizens has ever been raised. Perhaps this is because it is a touchy area, and people do hold very strong beliefs.

Over the years, I have sponsored a number of men. And I've always been struck by how, at some point, most of them will usually find some corner of their lives that can be justified as not being subject to the spiritual principles of the AA program: "AA's just for my alcoholism. I don't have to use it for [fill in the blank with your favorite untouchable issue]." I think what happened at our Friday evening meeting was that there were a number of politically committed individuals who unconsciously applied that to this area of their lives. The fact that "[fill in the blank with the name of the politician or presidential candidate you love to hate the most] is so wrong justifies my feelings and actions."

In revisiting what I might have done to help get the meeting back on track, I think that just mentioning the words "in all our affairs" might have helped. I think our program of recovery calls us to the highest level of civility and kindness we can muster, regardless of the topic at hand. I think that nothing is outside the bounds of the principles of our program. And that includes politics.

Anonymous
Tucson, Arizona

Fear, Suspicion, Distrust
MAY 1988 *(From Dear Grapevine)*

I got sober in a small town of 30,000, and for the first year I had a sobriety filled with fear, suspicion, and distrust. I am gay, and although I was uneasy in AA, fearing rejection, I also wanted to live and so made the choice to do the best I could with what I had. As I passed my first year, however, my fear and its sister, resentment, swelled to unbearable proportions. I joined World Hello (international correspondence group) looking for a "safe" place to dump my rage, and dump I did!

My outraged article was published in the newsletter, and within three weeks I was receiving letters from all over the world, begging me not to give up, encouraging me to extend my trust and assuring me that I was loved and accepted "as is." The overwhelming amount of caring given to me melted my walls, dissolving me into a flood of tears of relief and remorse. I came to realize that I was practicing with a vengeance the very sort of prejudice I had accused my home group of (not bothering to check the facts). I had been ready to scrap AA and all its people over the opinions of a very few. I was practicing the wholesale condemnation that I arrogantly claimed to hate in others. I began to examine my motives and came to the realization that I came to AA for help in staying sober—period—and I *had* been given that help, without a price tag, without having to change my beliefs. Who am I to demand that others see things "my way"?

Since that time, much has changed for me. Once I stopped expecting others to rearrange their feelings just for me, I was able to risk sharing more honestly, with surprising results. Many people at home accept me as just another recovering person, and I am grateful and content to have it so. I feel respected and a part of my home group and I'd never felt I belonged anywhere on earth before. What a great gift I was willing to throw away (along with my life) for the sake of self-pity and resentment!

K. D.
Lebanon, Pennsylvania

The Best of Times
JULY 2007 *(From Dear Grapevine)*

As I approached my thirtieth anniversary, I reflected on what it was like, what happened, and what I am like now.

In 1990, I was living in San Diego. One weekend, nine AA friends and I went camping in the desert. We reserved a group campsite at a state park and planned a campfire AA meeting after dinner. We also made great preparations to put on a "fashion review" after the meeting. Each person was to dress up as "what we were like."

What a spectacle! One guy had on a blue boa; another person wore pajamas; I wore one of my mother's hats, and so on. No one remembered to take a copy of the AA Preamble, so we all recited it in unison. Ten gay men in festive costumes chanted, "Alcoholics Anonymous is a Fellowship of men and women ..." By the time we finished, a Marine and his wife walked up to our campsite. We thought we were going to be arrested, but he asked, "Is this an AA meeting?" (Have you ever seen a boa wilt?) We said, "Yes." The couple asked, "May we join you?" We said, "Of course."

I look back on difficult times in sobriety and I can say nothing bad ever happened to me—I was sober. Things do happen, and life takes its course. I am able to get through the tough times and I can look forward to the best of times because of AA.

Doug H.
Charlotte, North Carolina

In Diversity Is Strength
APRIL 1982

'm writing to share some subjective impressions of the 1981 Illinois State Conference, and to give some feedback in thanks to all those who helped. The conference as a whole was a beautiful and meaningful experience to me, but I want to address myself to one specific new experience: the visible presence of gay people working in the conference. Both the gay hospitality suite and the two workshops were a great success. The suite was open most of Friday, Saturday, and Sunday. From eighty to a hundred visitors dropped in, about evenly mixed between straight and gay. We had a radio and a guitar. We made countless trips to the store for more coffee, pop, and munchies, and there was lots of laughter and joy and sharing.

But it was more than just one big party. About half of the gay visitors were from outside Chicago, many of them "loners" in their AA communities and glad there was a place to come to be with other gay alcoholics. One man with many years' sobriety used the suite for his first public admission within the Fellowship that he was gay. One gay woman from Chicago had never attended a gay meeting. And of course, familiar faces were there.

The sharing and growth were not limited to our gay guests. A straight farmer from southern Illinois stopped in. By all appearances, it was his first contact with gay people, and he mixed well. A straight woman shared a personal romantic problem at one of several meeting we held late at night—a problem she had felt uncomfortable about sharing at previous meetings. A straight alcoholism counselor came in to find out where meetings for gay patients were located in his area. Several straight men and women who sponsor gay people came to check out our literature and broaden their perspectives.

I don't mean to emphasize a straight/gay dichotomy—if anything, our experience there was the opposite. There was a real mix of people, and I was impressed to see how strong we AAs are in our unity and how beautiful in our diversity. Our visitors were evenly divided between men and women, and a broad range of races, ages, backgrounds, and localities was represented.

Our two alkathons were a success. They were not listed as gay, and this brought a mix of people who knew what was scheduled and people for whom it was a surprise. At the first alkathon, there was only one speaker, who talked about his need in early sobriety to share his whole history of how it was, and about the advice not to talk about "those things." He gave a good, well-rounded view of the importance of gay groups to him personally, and the importance to him of being honest about who he is.

The second alkathon was a panel. Four of us shared our diversified experience: Some sobered up in gay groups; some, in regular meetings; some attend gay groups a lot today; others do not. Altogether, we talked about thirty minutes, and left the last half hour for comments and questions.

To me, this was the most beautiful part of the gay-organized events that weekend. We had some good, intelligent questions, such as how to handle Twelfth Step calls from gay people and whether gay meetings are open to any AA. One straight man spoke of his discomfort when he first heard what this alkathon would be, and of his growing realization—through hearing the panelists—that "you wanted to get sober just like everyone else here." He ended by thanking us for sharing our lives so openly with him. It was beautiful to see his display of open-mindedness and growth as he struggled to be free of his own old ideas.

One visitor from far away talked of his gratitude that there was a gay hospitality suite, and his sense of isolation at the conference before he found us. Several non-gay people who were minorities in other ways (racial, religious) talked of the importance of group acceptance, and shared *their* feelings of isolation and of unity.

The man who had talked at the first alkathon probably put it best when he was recounting some of the above experiences: "And these are just the miracles you could see. Who knows how many other changes and little miracles took place?"

L. B.
Chicago, Illinois

Acceptance Is a Two-Way Street
APRIL 1985

The fiftieth anniversary of AA in 1985 is a time for sharing and for gratitude. For gay people in AA, and for AA as a whole, it can also be a time for much-needed reflection.

I'm a gay man, and I rejoice in the fact that AA was there one day in 1973 when I finally somehow decided to really try to stay sober that day with the help of some people in the program. They were also gay, and they didn't feel sorry for me, or make excuses for me, or even try to change me. They simply understood, and loved me just as I was. They told me things would get better if I kept coming back and if I learned about the AA program. They were so right!

When I got sober those many years ago, AA groups for gay men and lesbians were beginning to spring up here and there all over the country. Today, there are perhaps a thousand such groups, and many tens of thousands of us also go to regular nongay meetings. Gay/lesbian groups have for sure had their growing pains, and many in AA have felt the pain but not much of the joy of the explosive growth of gay involvement in the Fellowship.

During my early sobriety, I noticed that gays in AA tended to keep to themselves, and many "straights" in AA tended to see us as separatist and divisive. There was very little communication. My gay sponsor told me right off there is no such thing as "gay AA." There are gay groups of AA, he said, where "gays can feel more comfortable and relate better with a lot more honesty; but the AA program is the same everywhere."

That made good sense to me, and I did learn about AA and I managed to stay sober each day. But I also stayed rather closeted within my own gay meetings. When I went to regular meetings, I was quietly resentful because it seemed others were all talking about their wives, husbands, children, and all those heterosexual things. I had been taught from early childhood that being gay is sinful and unacceptable to society, and I had a great deal of difficulty seeing those straight people in AA as anything other than "society."

Slowly, as I grew in the program, I began to reach out to straight people just as I reached out to gay people. Slowly, many of my intense personal feelings of guilt, fear, and isolation began to fade. I began to see AA as truly a nonjudgmental program of personal recovery, and a fellowship of equals.

As AA moves into its second fifty years, I feel strongly that gay people should extend the hand of friendship to those in the Fellowship who do not know us very well. We can feel maligned if we wish. However, we do have one distinct advantage: Almost all of us grew up in heterosexual homes, but many straights in AA know very little about gays.

Lack of understanding breeds distrust and fear. But it's almost impossible, especially in AA, to distrust someone who stands right there beside you, loves you, and follows the path of sobriety with you. We should not *judge* one another. As the Big Book says, "God alone can judge our sex situation."

I have a lesbian friend in the program who says she wears "two hats, one for my involvement in AA and the other for my work in gay rights. I try my best not to wear my gay rights hat when doing my AA work. This is something we should all strive to do, whether it be politics, religion, or whatever. And it's my AA work that really tests me; politics is easy."

I was involved with a gay roundup recently which, despite the reservations of some, invited an AA area delegate (straight) to be a panelist at a workshop on gay meetings/straight meetings. The result was a great deal of learning and a joyful opening of the doors of communication. A gay special international group within AA was joined at its meeting a few weeks ago by a member of the AA board of trustees; the love and mutual understanding which flowed from that meeting was remarkable.

My own home group invited nongay AAs to help us with workshops on service and on unity and the Traditions, and other gay/lesbian groups I attend have had great meetings by inviting nongay speakers.

I've heard a gay old-timer, with a lot more years than I have, offer this advice many times to gay AAs: "Resentments and isolation are what kill us drunks, and service and love are what help keep us alive and well. Acceptance is a two-way street. Volunteer to answer the phones at central office and ask to be put on the Twelfth Step list if you're ready. And make sure your group contributes to central office and to the General Service Office. If you don't have a GSR (general service representative), elect one. The same goes for a central office representative and a Grapevine representative. Get involved, damn it. Get into action!"

For me, the most vital thing in AA is unity. Without unity AA could never have flourished and grown for fifty years to carry its message of hope and recovery to suffering alcoholics of every type imaginable, everywhere. Including me.

P. J.
Los Angeles, California

Special Interest Groups?
APRIL 1989 *(Excerpt from Dear Grapevine)*

I have successfully been with the AA program since January, 1975, and will admit that the glory and wonder were slow to come at first but now, my cup overflows and it keeps coming as long as I stay out of the way.

There has been as much gay material in Grapevine as has been contributed, I am sure, but bearing in mind that we are in AA to get and stay sober I like to see the focus of the material deal with the disease of alcoholism and not other problems and addictions.

I am gay. When I go to meetings I freely talk about how drinking affected my relationships with my partner of many years. The other people at the meetings talk about the same things and they aren't gay. I believe the problem arises when we try to force-feed people on the virtues of homosexuality, forgetting that we are whole people. Most of the "straight" people I know are not really interested in me as a homosexual and wouldn't be interested in me at all if that were the obsessive image I chose to project.

Gay meetings have their place and help a great many people get started in the program, but I strongly recommend breaking the mold, by becoming a whole person, by being open, kind, and honest everywhere.

B. J.
Lyndeborough, New Hampshire

Love and Tolerance
NOVEMBER 1996

For the first couple of years of my sobriety, one of my mainstay meetings was a noontime group that met daily. My drinking pattern toward the end had been to start drinking around noon and that meeting gave me a real sense of security. The couches were seedy, the room was dingy, the meeting was sometimes quite small, but it was home. Most of the regulars had less than a year, so sometimes the discussion focused more on problems than solutions, but there were a few people with three years or more who tried to keep us focused on living the AA way of life.

One day a newcomer showed up and sat in the corner, away from everyone else. He seemed a bit more fearful and apprehensive than the average newcomer. When the leader called on him to share, he said, "My name is Daniel and I'm an alcoholic." He proceeded to talk about how the church he belonged to and the God he believed in strongly condemned homosexuals and that the fate of all homosexuals was eternal damnation. Such reference to sectarian religious doctrine and the expression of an opinion on an outside issue would be out of place in any AA meeting, but since this was a gay group, his comments were particularly inappropriate. As he continued to share along these lines, many group members became visibly uncomfortable, and some even got up and left. Our safe space had been violated.

Daniel continued to come to the meeting for the next few days and to share along these same lines. It created quite an uproar in the group; some regulars simply stopped attending, and others wanted to kick Daniel out. For some reason, his tirades didn't bother me, but I was perplexed. Why was this man, who so obviously couldn't tolerate gays, coming to this group? Was it because he was on some crusade to "save" us? And how should the group respond to him? I was one year sober at the time and didn't yet have a good working knowledge of the Traditions, so I sat on the sidelines and observed as a couple of those three-year-plus members, one of whom was my sponsor, took control of the situation.

They began to spend some time after the meeting talking with Daniel. They'd noticed something in him that perhaps the rest of us had missed—that he desperately wanted to stay sober. Mixed in with his anti-gay message, he talked about the same things all new-comers talk about—how alcohol had ruined his life, how hard it was to stay away from the first drink, and how he had come to AA for help. My sponsor and the others told Daniel that he was welcome at our meeting, but that he needed to keep his sharing focused on his alcoholism rather than on his attitudes toward gays. They did this gently but firmly. And they asked him questions about his particular case. As they learned more about Daniel, they discovered something that many of us had begun to suspect. Daniel was one who suffered from grave emotional and mental disorders, and part of his problem was a learning disability. He had only learned one bus route, and the only meeting place that he knew on that bus route was ours. He wasn't coming to our meeting with the express purpose of disrupting it and "saving" us homosexuals from ourselves. He was coming to our meeting because it was the only one he knew how to get to, and he wanted sobriety so badly that he was willing to sit in a room full of people he had been taught to hate and fear in order to hear the message of AA. Here was a man who was truly willing to go to any lengths to stay sober.

Once my sponsor and the others discovered Daniel's problem they knew exactly what to do. They got some bus schedules and a meeting schedule. They selected a meeting place nearby that had a number of mainstream meetings every day and plotted out the route and the transfers that Daniel would need to take to get to these meetings. And they went with him the first time to make sure he didn't get lost. They never tried to lecture him or to change his beliefs. They simply treated him like they would any other new-comer who needed some extra guidance.

I don't know what became of Daniel, but I do know that I learned a lot about the Traditions from watching the way in which our more experienced members responded to this situation. I learned that even though we were a special interest group, we were first and foremost an AA group, whose primary purpose was to carry the message of AA to this alcoholic, who so desperately wanted it. I learned that because the only requirement for membership is a desire to stop drinking, no group has the right to kick someone out of a meeting, and because of the First Tradition the group must respond to a member who is disruptive or else the unity of the group could suffer. We were fortunate to have some members who knew how to respond to this disruption in the full spirit of our First Tradition: "AA must continue to live or most of us will surely die. Hence, our common welfare comes first. But individual welfare follows close afterward."

Joel C.
San Diego, California

There Is Only One AA

NOVEMBER 1984 *(From Dear Grapevine)*

I live in a city with a large gay population, many of whom are recovering alcoholics in AA. I surrendered to my alcoholism in January 1980 and was sent to a gay-oriented AA meeting by a treatment program. For months, the only meetings I attended were gay—that's what I needed at the time.

After a few months, an old-timer in one of the groups suggested that I try one of the mixed meetings. I resisted at first. I was scared. But one day, asking God for courage, I walked into an AA club downtown. I really believed that someone would ask me to leave. I was even afraid they would ask me to prove I was a true alcoholic, whatever that is. But nothing happened except that I attended a very good AA meeting and was given a whole lot of self-confidence and a little positive pride in myself for taking that risk.

After a few weeks, some of the secretaries even asked me to chair meetings. I made new friends. I heard new points of view on the Steps and on daily recovery. The most important thing I heard, though, was the sharing. Even though I couldn't identify with all of the particulars, I could identify with the pain, loneliness, fear, and misery other alcoholics described. I could identify when someone, gay or straight, shared a living problem and how it was dealt with through AA.

Today, as a result of attending both gay and other meetings, I am a happier alcoholic. My circle of friends has expanded tremendously. When I hear the terms "straight AA" or "gay AA," I cringe. They are a myth. There is only one AA, "a fellowship of men and women who share their experience, strength and hope with each other that they may solve their common problem and help others to recover from alcoholism."

J. C.
San Francisco, California

You Are Not Done Yet
MARCH 2009

I came to AA in 1996 after my second DUI. Encouraged by my attorney to take an action before going to court, I immediately started attending AA meetings.

I soon became aware of just how out of control my life had become after 13 years of boozing. I got a sponsor and began working the First Step. Wow, I thought. This is exactly what my life is like—completely unmanageable. My finances were a disaster, friends were nearly non-existent, my communication with family had deteriorated to the rare holiday call and I felt trapped in the misery of an unhealthy relationship and a job I loathed.

At the same time, I was noticing that those who had been around AA for a while seemed to have order in their lives. I wanted what they had, but that would have meant quitting my job and leaving my eight-year relationship. People kept telling me not to make any major changes in the first year. I listened, waited, and worked the program. My sponsor kept telling me, "It's a process!" I grew to hate the phrase, but he was so right!

As I put together more time, things started to become a bit more orderly. I spoke with the IRS and established a payment plan for those five years of claiming 14 dependents, I gradually reintroduced myself to my family, and I started to make friends in AA. I stayed at my job and with my partner until I was sober for one year and eight months. As a result of making meetings, working the Steps and a whole lot of prayer, something clicked at that point in my sobriety. I took everything I owned (my clothes and two television sets) and left my partner. I accepted a new job that paid a salary of less than half of what I had previously been making, but with a lot less stress. The changes were scary, but I knew without doubt that they were good for my sobriety, my spirituality and my serenity. I rented a room from someone in the program for $75 a month. I cut back and survived on peanut butter sandwiches and water, but it was okay: I was happy in my journey. I knew that as long as I did not drink and continued going to meetings, everything would be okay, no matter how bad things might seem.

The "process" continued and after six months I was recruited by another company in my new field. Suddenly I was earning the same amount of money I had made in my previous career. Within a year, I had found my own place, a small studio apartment in the heart of Washington, D.C., close to work and, more importantly, lots of meetings.

As I continued to clean up the wreckage of the past, I put a concerted effort into establishing stability in all areas of my life, and after about four years of sober time, I had my little place, my cat Chad, many dear friends, a job I loved and my sobriety.

In my daily prayer and meditation, without fail, I would ask God to continue to bring good into my life. Over the course of the next two years, I had a number of suitors, but I was happy in my little life. I had a chance to move to a bigger place, but my place was comfortable and safe. I was invited to join others for activities, but I did not want to rock the boat. My life was manageable and I intended to keep it that way.

Unmanageability is horrible, but too much manageability is the same as taking control and not letting God's will be done.

In February 2002, just after my six-year sober anniversary, my boss approached me and said she was planning on opening a new office in New York City; she said she would like me to go there and work. Of course, I immediately said, "No!" I couldn't leave my meetings, my friends or my orderly little life. She asked me to think about it over the weekend and get back to her; I agreed.

Well, needless to say, HP and I did some heavy talking that weekend. As I prayed to him to bring good into my life, he interrupted me! He said, "What do you think I have been trying to do? But you keep shutting the door on it! The suitors, the opportunities, to all of them you have said no. Do you really want me to bring good into your life, or do you want to keep this simple, overly managed little existence that you have? It is a process and you are not done yet!" Whoa, I thought, he's right!

I relocated to New York City in December 2002. I immediately started doing 90 meetings in 90 days, I got a sponsor and I got a sponsee. I made a commitment to myself and my Higher Power that I would take the first service position that came my way. One of my AA friends was in need of a co-chair for the fund-raising committee of the Big Apple Roundup. I first thought this was more than I'd asked for, but I kept my promise and said, "Sign me up!"

This service position was truly God-given; it took me to meetings all over the city, from Queens to the Bronx, even to Long Island. I got to plan sober events and to get others involved as well, especially newcomers. My process was back in motion After six months, one of my suitors from D.C., with my blessing, moved to New York to be with me.

After two years as a New Yorker, hundreds of new friends and acquaintances, and a life experience beyond my wildest dreams, my partner decided city life wasn't for him. He wanted to move to Florida. I was at first disappointed, but then I remembered my prayer, and posted my resume online to see what might happen. Within six weeks, we moved to Fort Lauderdale.

Today my partner and I have a wonderful home on the water that we share with our Dalmatian and two cats. I have an incredible job. I live within a few hours of my mother and my brother's family. I have returned to college and will soon finish my bachelor's degree. I have a fantastic home group. Although my time in New York ended abruptly, it was an excellent adventure that I nearly missed out on. I made lifelong friends and found some of the best AA I have ever encountered.

The most important idea I have learned during this "process" is that a lot of good can come from change. I learned that I need to listen to my Higher Power. I learned not to fear that which God puts in my path. I learned that unmanageability is horrible, but that too much manageability is the same as taking control and not letting God's will be done.

Today, I pray to God to continue to bring good into my life. Then slowly, I open my eyes, anticipating just what exciting adventure he may have in store for me next!

Patrick F.
Fort Lauderdale, Florida

THE TWELVE STEPS

1. We admitted we were powerless over alcohol—that our lives had become unmanageable.
2. Came to believe that a Power greater than ourselves could restore us to sanity.
3. Made a decision to turn our will and our lives over to the care of God *as we understood Him.*
4. Made a searching and fearless moral inventory of ourselves.
5. Admitted to God, to ourselves, and to another human being the exact nature of our wrongs.
6. Were entirely ready to have God remove all these defects of character.
7. Humbly asked Him to remove our shortcomings.
8. Made a list of all persons we had harmed, and became willing to make amends to them all.
9. Made direct amends to such people wherever possible, except when to do so would injure them or others.
10. Continued to take personal inventory and when we were wrong promptly admitted it.
11. Sought through prayer and meditation to improve our conscious contact with God *as we understood Him,* praying only for knowledge of His will for us and the power to carry that out.
12. Having had a spiritual awakening as the result of these steps, we tried to carry this message to alcoholics, and to practice these principles in all our affairs.

THE TWELVE TRADITIONS

1. Our common welfare should come first; personal recovery depends upon A.A. unity.
2. For our group purpose there is but one ultimate authority—a loving God as He may express Himself in our group conscience. Our leaders are but trusted servants; they do not govern.
3. The only requirement for A.A. membership is a desire to stop drinking.
4. Each group should be autonomous except in matters affecting other groups or A.A. as a whole.
5. Each group has but one primary purpose—to carry its message to the alcoholic who still suffers.
6. An A.A. group ought never endorse, finance or lend the A.A. name to any related facility or outside enterprise, lest problems of money, property and prestige divert us from our primary purpose.
7. Every A.A. group ought to be fully self-supporting, declining outside contributions.
8. Alcoholics Anonymous should remain forever nonprofessional, but our service centers may employ special workers.
9. A.A., as such, ought never be organized; but we may create service boards or committees directly responsible to those they serve.
10. Alcoholics Anonymous has no opinion on outside issues; hence the A.A. name ought never be drawn into public controversy.
11. Our public relations policy is based on attraction rather than promotion; we need always maintain personal anonymity at the level of press, radio and films.
12. Anonymity is the spiritual foundation of all our traditions, ever reminding us to place principles before personalities.

Alcoholics Anonymous

AA's program of recovery is fully set forth in its basic text, *Alcoholics Anonymous* (commonly known as the Big Book), now in its Fourth Edition, as well as in *Twelve Steps and Twelve Traditions*, *Living Sober*, and other books. Information on AA can also be found on AA's website at www.AA.ORG, or by writing to:

Alcoholics Anonymous
Box 459
Grand Central Station
New York, NY 10163

For local resources, check your local telephone directory under "Alcoholics Anonymous." Four pamphlets, "This is A.A.," "Is A.A. For You?," "44 Questions," and "A Newcomer Asks" are also available from AA.

AA Grapevine

AA Grapevine is AA's international monthly journal, published continuously since its first issue in June 1944. The AA pamphlet on AA Grapevine describes its scope and purpose this way: "As an integral part of Alcoholics Anonymous since 1944, the Grapevine publishes articles that reflect the full diversity of experience and thought found within the A.A. Fellowship, as does La Viña, the bimonthly Spanish-language magazine, first published in 1996. No one viewpoint or philosophy dominates their pages, and in determining content, the editorial staff relies on the principles of the Twelve Traditions."

In addition to magazines, AA Grapevine, Inc. also produces books, eBooks, audiobooks, and other items. It also offers a Grapevine Online subscription, which includes: five new stories weekly, AudioGrapevine (the audio version of the magazine), Grapevine Story Archive (the entire collection of Grapevine articles), and the current issue of Grapevine and La Viña in HTML format. For more information on AA Grapevine, or to subscribe to any of these, please visit the magazine's website at www.AAGRAPEVINE.ORG or write to:

AA Grapevine, Inc.
475 Riverside Drive
New York, NY 10115